Miklós M. Molnár

33
HUNGARIAN
HISTORIES

HUNGARIAN IDENTITY
THROUGH PORTRAITS

Published by Catch Budapest in 2018.

ISBN 978-1-71775-367-0

www.CatchBudapest.com

Table of Contents

Preface

Hungary's saga sparkles with tales of brilliant individuals whose derring-do and perseverance shaped the essential spirit of modern Magyar existence, often changing the course of world history in the process. From nomadic warriors of the Dark Ages to refined adventurers of Europe's nobility to scientific luminaries launching into the Atomic Era, generations of notable Hungarians frequently overcome ever-daunting adversities to achieve planet-shaking accomplishments – all while living out colorfully exuberant existences that can make the wildest fiction seem tame.

As one of these venturesome Magyars who pursues dreams while enhancing reality, Miklós Molnár is an astute observer of history as it happens, with a wholehearted appreciation for the heroes of Hungary's past and present. As a teacher, translator, and international tour guide, Miklós continually brings together countless lives in his native country and on his global travels; as an expressive writer with a uniquely sagacious sense of perception, Miklós is extraordinarily suited to encapsulate the most momentous accounts of Hungary's greatest historical figures, including many whose efforts have gone largely unsung.

This chronicle of 33 remarkable figures from throughout Hungarian history will captivate aficionados of Magyar culture, while offering the casual reader insight to the many worldly contributions brought forth by Hungary's brightest stars. Miklós sheds light upon his subjects with an uncannily incisive blend of gripping narrative and good humor, utilizing a lighthearted voice of respectful reverence that makes him an excellent storyteller and convivial company – the perfect person to share exhilarating anecdotes of Hungary's idiosyncratic souls.

NICK ROBERTSON
Editor in Chief - Where Budapest Magazine

How to Read this Book (Preface by the Author)

> *"HUNGARY. A mania (med. fixa idea) with a population of ten million. It is now generally regarded as curable, though this would take away much of its charm."*

István Örkény

The purpose of this collection of portraits is to initiate the outsider to Hungarianness, to show from a Hungarian point of view what kind of people our culture produced in different periods of time in history and thus what Örkény meant by "its charm."

Once a Hungarian, always a Hungarian. Just like the accent, one cannot drop it. Being a Hungarian is rather a mode of existence developed by centuries in pursuit of surviving at the cross-roads of great power interests. Though I would not go as far as Arthur Koestler who claimed that " ...to be a Hungarian is a collective neurosis," after reading these sketches, lives cramped into 600 words, the reader will have to admit that being a Hungarian is at least an adventure.

We, Hungarians, are a pretty self-content people. We tend to be proud of being Hungarian, speaking a unique language, surviving history against all odds, producing 'world famous' talents. At the same time we feel isolated (see language), victims of history (suffering from 'historical wounds') and not recognized by the rest of the world (how come you don't know that Houdini was Hungarian as well?).

Problems start when we go abroad and have to identify ourselves. Even if we speak a foreign language (most Hungarians don't) we soon become perplexed when others cannot place us on the map, some more informed tend to think that the 'hungry people's' capital is Bucharest, which we take as an insult. And it's very easy to insult us since in spite of all the self-pride, Hungarians suffer from an inferiority complex. We want to be recognized as equal to the most civilized nations. A negative remark made about Hungary in a no-name newspaper in America, Germany or France generates headline news and hysterical reactions. Perhaps it's because our national pride is based on living in a historical haze. What's conquest for others is 'home taking' for us, what we call the 'adventures of the Hungarians in the 10th century' is brutally called 'raids' in English.

The life stories of the 33 people that follows are meant to be typical examples of how location and historical context can shape individual fates. Even those who left Hungary are good examples since they had a reason to leave, let it be political persecution or personal choice. The selection of who is among the 33 is definitely not representative of either Hungarian historical figures or geniuses of arts and sciences. If there is a common denominator, it's their Hungarianness, let them be statesmen, geniuses of arts or just vagabonds.

After reading some or all of these pieces and become more familiar with Hungary today you may come to the conclusion that Örkény was wrong in one thing: being Hungarian is incurable after all.

In Search of Roots

Attila the Hun, Our Hun

Mór Than's painting "The Feast of Attila" based on a fragment of Priscus

Left: The Empire of the Huns and subject tribes at the time of Attila.
Right: Allegorical depiction by Eugène Delacroix (1843–1847) – Title: Attila and his Hordes Overrun Italy and the Arts (detail).

Every 7th of January I have to call four friends called Attila and congratulate them on their name day. A Hungarian table calendar tells you whose name day it is, and just to make sure, every morning the radio announcer congratulates those who are celebrating their name day. In addition, a little sign at the florist's reminds of the name day, just in case you forgot. Though less in fashion than in earlier decades, name days are still a good excuse for boozing and fraternizing in this country. The paradox of the Attila name day is that originally name days were an Orthodox Christian tradition, but Attila the Hun was neither Christian nor Hungarian.

What's his role in this book then? The short answer is: it's a long story. Actually, two parallel stories. One is the real historical version, the other, a colourful pool of legends and myths, the products of later centuries spiced with contemporary special effects. The latter is more interesting. Nevertheless, let's stick first to the real Attila.

The real story starts with the nomadic Huns roaming from the steppes of Inner Asia and reaching the Carpathian basin in the early 5th century. They consolidated their power by making conquered tribes their loyal vassals. Like all nomadic invaders (including the Hungarian tribes arriving in the present territory in the 9th century) they had one sole objective: to maintain their superiority by raiding and looting, while keeping people in constant fear of their military skill through a style of fighting unknown to their enemies.

Born the child of Hun Chief Mundzuk in 406, Attila only came to power at the age of 28, when his father's brother, King Ruga, died suddenly when he was struck by lightning.

His elder brother Bleda inherited the title, but according to Hunnic tradition they shared power, at least until Bleda's death in unknown circumstances in 445. Their eleven-year rule was a major blow for the Eastern Roman Empire. After rampaging in the Balkans, the Hunnic armies got as near as the fortified walls of Constantinople, where they negotiated three peace agreements that resulted in the Huns being well supplied with gold and riches.

The dual kingship ended with Bleda's death, and for the next eight years Attila assumed sole power over the Huns and their subordinated peoples. Of the two brothers Attila was more the warrior type and more ambitious. Looking to further expand his empire Attila soon terminated the agreement made by his uncle Ruga with the Romans, and started his long march to the western part of Europe, leaving no cities unharmed. At the peak of his rule, the short-lived Hunnic Empire extended from the Baltic to as far as the Atlantic; the devastation he brought to the west created the basis for his mythical image as, "the scourge of God". Attila's unexpected death due to internal bleeding in 453 left the peoples of Europe in disarray; his three sons (Ellak, Denghizik and Ernak) were unable to hold the vast empire together, and in absence of a charismatic leader like Attila, the vassal tribes soon seceded. Atilla's appearance on the 5th c. European scene represented a fatal blow to the Latin Roman Empire, which came to an inglorious end, opening the way for the formation of western Christian nations.

This is the historians' dry version of Attila's life and the role he played. More important is his mythical rebirth. Since authentic sources about his life are so scarce, his character is ideal for the creation of legends and myths. Western (German, French and Italian) popular literature portrays Attila as the epitome of Eastern barbarism, with dog's ears, he was a cruel, merciless warrior, the archenemy of anything civilized.

Hungarians on the contrary have their own story and it is deeply ingrained in our national consciousness due to literary works and those who ardently oppose the Finno-Ugrian theory concerning the origin of the Hungarians. Since Hungarians are obsessed with their ethnic genealogy, especially the Asian links, there are innumerable camps of those who believe in the various theories, and it's useless to argue with them. The circle of legends connected to the Huns and in particular to Attila is so widely taken for granted that it would be equivalent to a betrayal of the nation to say that all these myths are just the products of the vivid imaginations of a few chroniclers. To name just a few, here is a short list of the most common beliefs attached to Attila and the Huns:

The Huns and the Hungarians are practically the same nation (never mind the 400 years between the 460s when the Huns disappeared and the year 896 when Hungarian tribes under Chief Árpád conquered the Carpathian Basin). Some believers of the theory claim that Árpád is a direct blood descendant of Attila.

Contrary to the western view, Attila was a humane and wise ruler in the eyes of most Hungarians, even sparing Rome from destruction at the request of Pope Leo I.

Attila a popular first name, and other Hunnic characters also have domesticated Hungarian names, "Bleda" becoming "Buda" for example, the city being named after him.

The weirdest extreme you can reach in myth making is the case of prince Csaba, who is claimed by the Székely people living in Transylvania to be Attila's son. This would make the Székelys direct descendants of the Huns. Finally, it's an ongoing national game to find Attila's grave at the bottom of a river where he was buried in three coffins, one gold, one silver and one iron.

No matter what historians and western image distorters say, Attila is great and he is ours, insofar as other peoples from the steppes have a claim too, and a lot of Turkish babies receive "Attila" as their first name, as well. Nevertheless, myth-making on such a large scale has also a boomerang effect: people are punished for believing what the myth-makers produced both in the West and the East. The figure of Attila will provide excellent ammunition for both second-rate Hollywood filmmakers and self-claimed researchers of our Asian roots for centuries to come.

Chief Árpád, The Founding Father

"Honfoglalás" by Mihály Munkácsy

Left: Árpád's statue on Heroes' Square (Budapest)
Right: Statue of Árpád at Ráckeve (Town in Hungary)

Have you ever been on a guided tour of Heroes' Square? A nightmare for tour guides and guaranteed mental exhaustion for tourists to digest a thousand-years' history of Hungary in 15 minutes. What might remain in your memory are the oversized figures of seven scary tribal chiefs with slit eyes on fine horses with Árpád in the centre. They are the euphemistically called "home-takers" as all Hungarian school children learn about them at a very early age, never mind textbooks in the neighboring countries or western historiography that label them as conquerors.

The composition is monumental, echoing the spirit of the 1896 Millennial Celebrations when it was unveiled. The underlying idea is to convey the message of Hungarian cultural and political supremacy in the region, a myth polished to perfection through the centuries. Though the myth is still virile and dear to most Hungarians, it should not be dismissed as a manifestation of Hungarian nationalism. The story of Árpád and his occupation of the land is so well-rounded and moving that you would not want to argue with it for some iconoclastic historical revision. So, here is the story:

The ethnogenesis of the myth of the Hungarians finding their homeland goes back to Emese's dream. Árpád's grandmother had a dream in which a bird of prey called 'turul,' a totem animal of the tribe, delivered a divine message that from her womb a great river would begin and flow to strange lands. The shamans interpreted it to mean that her descendants would be kings who would lead their people to a final homeland.

The son, named Álmos, became indeed the one who united the seven tribes into a confederacy, sealed by a blood covenant while they were still in Etelköz, located around the rivers Dnieper and Dniester North of the Black Sea. Due to the threatening Pechenegs the Hungarian tribes were forced to move westward by the 890s. Álmos, by now an old man, was replaced by his son Árpád who organized and led the resettlement of the whole population (around 200.000 people) to the present territory of Hungary through the Verecke pass in the Carpathian mountains in 895. According to legend, after their arrival he sent a white horse with golden harness to Svatopluk, the Moravian ruler of the region, as a gift. In exchange, Árpád asked for a bucket of water, a piece of earth and a tuft of green grass, a request that Svatopluk was happy to fulfill. Being ignorant of the symbolism used by the people of the steppe he realized too late that he had handed over his land with its rivers to the newcomers, thus the Hungarians were justified later when they claimed they had a right to the land. It took Árpád only twelve years to consolidate power over the whole Carpathian basin after the decisive Hungarian victory over the Bavarian forces at Pressburg (Bratislava) in 907.

The Árpád of the legends seems to satisfy the need of all Hungarians to have a father figure who led our ancestors to this land of Paradise, in the same vein as Moses did with his people. Lacking reliable sources, what can be known about the real Árpád for sure, is the date of his death in 907, when he must have been around 60 years old. Though we have no record of his wife's name, thanks to Byzantine sources we know the names of his five children. Though it is disputed whether his youngest son Zolta followed him as Grand Prince, it's for sure that the dynasty he established, the

House of Árpád, ruled for four centuries until 1301 when the last of the dynasty, András III, died without an heir.

Though there are hardly two historians to be found who would agree on the details of the home taking, the legendary figure of Árpád seems to have set firm in the minds of Hungarians. No matter if foreign sources, especially in the neighbouring countries, label the events as a conquest, Hungarians are undeterred from visualizing it as our late 19th century painter Mihály Munkácsy depicted it in his monumental painting *Honfoglalás*, one of the major sights in the Hungarian Parliament.

Sándor Kőrösi-Csoma, Seeking Hungarian roots, founding Tibetology

Left: Lithography showing Sándor Kőrösi-Csoma by Schöfft Ágoston
Right: Tomb and Memorial in a cemetery of Darjeeling, often garlanded with khatas

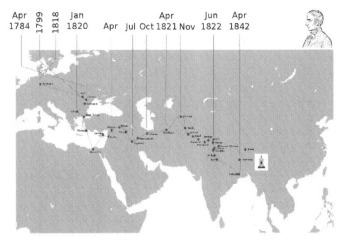

Route taken by Sándor Kőrösi-Csoma

In 2007 a young architect named Balázs Irimiás visited Zangla, a faraway place in Kashmir. There he found a deserted Tibetan monastery in ruins.

184 years before, another Hungarian had visited the same monastery. He spent over a year in a small unheated room surrounded by books and manuscripts on Tibetan literature and religion. For sixteen months he supped yak butter tea, and wrapped up in woollen sheets to keep warm. This man was Kőrösi Csoma Sándor, the future founder of Tibetology. Touched by the spirit of the monastery, the young architect started a "buy a brick" campaign to raise funds for its refurbishment.

But what was it that drove Kőrösi Csoma to leave his beloved Transylvania for the Orient at the age of 35?

The explanation lies in the Hungarians' obsession with their ethnic origins. When Hungarians abroad are asked where they are from, they often feel humiliated. It's not the occasional jibe that we must be "hungry". It's more that we feel we lack recognition – people struggle to put us on the map. For the proud Magyars, being labeled as Slavic or German is a major insult. We are from Asia, not Europe.

However, Magyar origins can only be traced back accurately to Árpád, the 9th century chief who led the Magyars to the Carpathian Basin. Beyond that, speculation on our ethnic origins has spawned some bizarre theories, including a dubious connection with the Sumerians. Now, according to linguistic and ethnographic research, the view is that we are of Finno-Ugric stock, and that's official. But in Kőrösi Csoma's time, little was known of our eastern origins. Then, many thought we are descendants of the Huns (even today,

Attila is a popular name in Hungary). Another theory suggested that Hungarian is linked to the Uyghur language. Thus, Kőrösi Csoma set out to find the true origins of the Hungarians. His final destination, which he was never to reach, was Uyghuristan in Northern China.

He set off on his long journey in 1819. Three years later he reached Ladakh, at the foot of the Himalayas. On his way he passed through Istanbul, Alexandria, Baghdad, and Tehran – where he left his passport. He went on without documentation to Bokhara, Kabul, Lahore and finally Kashmir. There he met William Moorcroft, an explorer for the East India Company. Moorcroft changed the course of Csoma's life by persuading him to study Tibetan. Csoma relished the opportunity, hoping to find references to Hungarian in ancient Tibetan scripts. Moorcroft arranged for Csoma to stay with the Lama of Yangla, and commissioned him to compile a Tibetan-English dictionary, the first of its kind. This is how Csoma ended up in the monastery. Ten years later, his Tibetan grammar and dictionary was published in Calcutta, bringing him academic recognition. But Csoma did not stop searching for the origins of the Magyars. He later learnt Sanskrit – one of 17 languages he mastered – only to find it was another cul-de-sac in his quest. In 1842 he left for Lhasa, the Tibetan capital, in a search for sources on the Uyghurs. However, he contracted malaria in Darjeeling, and died at the age of 58. Ever since, his tomb has been a place of pilgrimage for Hungarians visiting India.

Today schools and streets are named after him. His unrelenting pursuit of his goals and his faith in the Hungarian idea that "We are people of the Orient" – despite all the hardship and humiliation he endured – means he stands proud in the canon of Hungarian heroes.

The Csoma's Room project, run by Balázs Irimiás, is just another example of how deeply the Asian connection is rooted in Hungarian national identity.

Ármin Vámbéry, The Dervish in Disguise

Left: Portrait of Ármin Vámbéry
Right: Bust at Hungarian Geographical Museum in Érd

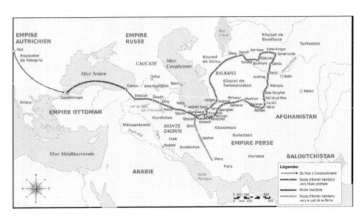

Map of the travels of Armin Vambery in Central Asia

My Turkish friend in Istanbul insists that Hungarians are just another Turkish tribe; at least, that's what they were taught at school. No wonder the 'madjar' tourist gets a most favourable treatment in the bazaar. However, Hungarian textbooks still teach that, until the defeat of the Hungarians by the Suleiman the Magnificent at Mohács in 1526, Hungary was as prosperous as England and all our subsequent misery and decline is to be blamed on the 150-year Turkish yoke. Hungarian heroism in fighting the "pagan" Turks is a matter of national pride.

The person who shed light on the ongoing debate about our Turkish roots was a charismatic figure of Hungarian social science, Ármin Vámbéry. He was known in Muslim countries as Rasid Effendi, meaning the honourable man of letters. His 81-year lifespan was a testament to will over circumstances. Armed with a sense of mission, raw talent and iron will, he overcame the barriers of poverty and handicap to attain great achievements.

Right after his birth in 1832 his father died of cholera, and since Jews were exempt from birth certificates, he was never sure of his birthday. He was brought up as Hermann Wamberger in Dunaszerdahely (Dunajska Streda, Slovakia), a city of orthodox Jews at the time. At the age of three he contracted inflammatory arthritis of the hip and became lame in his left leg for the rest of his life. From then on his life was a series of struggles as his 400-page autobiography published in 1905, *The Story of My Struggles*, suggests.

Thanks to his exceptional memorization skills he soon excelled as a polyglot genius during his haphazard schooling at the local yeshiva and then at Calvinist and Catholic grammar schools in Bratislava. He earned his bread and tuition by tutoring from a very early age but after getting frustrated by the humiliation he had to suffer due to his poverty and Jewishness he soon left formal education and became his own tutor learning one language after another. By the age of 25 he spoke almost as many languages as the number of his years.

Vámbéry became obsessed with learning Turkish which became the turning point of his life and career. At a time when the Finno-Ugrian origin of our ancient tongue was still not proven scientifically, he soon found influential sponsors among the literary elite and set off to Turkey to study. During his four-year stay in Istanbul he not only mastered his knowledge of Turkish to perfection but through his erudite knowledge of the Koran he made his way to the highest circles of the Ottoman Court. Driven by an inexhaustible thirst for knowledge he decided to search for the Asian roots of Hungarians, which he assumed were in the steppes of Central Asia.

What later brought him world fame and confirmed him as the top authority in matters of the Orient was his 9-month long sojourn in 1863 to the kaganates of Central Asia; the ruins of the great empire from the 14th century of Timur Lenk (Tamerlane). A journey to the forbidden cities of Bokhara, Samarkand and Khiva could have been a suicide mission. However, Vámbéry cleverly disguised himself as a Sunni dervish and mingled among the pilgrims of a caravan returning from Mecca to their homeland. So successful was his camouflage that he not only gained the trust of his fellow hadjis but managed to escape the interrogation of the emirs and even lectured them on the interpretation of the Koran. There was only one incident when he was almost found out on the way back in Afghanistan when the crown prince noticed that he was tapping his leg to the rhythm of the western-type military music. Ultimately he achieved what he wanted and collected enormous ethnographic and linguistic material from these ancient societies before they vanished a few decades later due to Russian conquest.

Upon his return to Pest he encountered difficulties in proving his theory of the Turkish origin of the Hungarian language since by then the defenders of the Finno-Ugrian line had won the battle. Shattered in his failure, but still resolute, he went to London where he published *Travels in Central Asia*. This brought him not only fame but access to the British political elite, including Queen Victoria. Through these connections he warned the British of the imminent Russian expansion in Central Asia and thus their threat to British interests in India.

At the age of 35 he became chair of Turkology at Budapest University where he would work until retirement in 1904 at the age of 72. Taking no political role or jobs he managed to maintain his integrity as a professor who educated younger generations of Orientology students. Despite his quiet life as an academic he continued to be consulted by British Prime Ministers and Turkish Sultans.

Vivid ethnographic descriptions and authentic insights into Asian culture make Vámbéry's work engaging even today. His clarity and charisma make his life's work most enviable to any travel writer, most certainly this one.

Nation Builders

Mátyás, The King in Disguise

Left: Portrait Matthias Corvinus
Right: Matthias Corvinus depicted in the *Chronica Hungarorum*

Matthias Corvinus Monument in front of St. Michael's Church in Cluj-Napoca, Romania

The personage of the fifteenth century King Matthias (Mátyás in Hungarian, Matei Corvin for Romanians) has been a bone of contention between Hungarians and Romanians for ages. Gheorghe Funar, the Hungarian bashing Romanian mayor of Kolozsvár (Cluj-Napoca) in the 1990s took the claim of Romanian history textbooks that Mátyás was of Romanian origin literally, and deleted Hungarian references from the statue of Mátyás in the main square of the city, causing a lot of inter-ethnic conflict.

True, Kolozsvár was the birthplace of Mátyás, whose father, János Hunyadi (Ioan de Hunedoara), Voivode of Transylvania (1440–1456) and Regent-Governor (1446–1453) of the Kingdom of Hungary traced his ancestry back to Wallachia (Old Romania). Nevertheless, the irrational ethnic rivalry of latter centuries would hardly have made any sense in the 15th century. Hunyadi wrote himself into the history books by his decisive victory over the advancing Ottomans at Nándorfehérvár (today Belgrade) in 1456, which delayed the Turkish conquest for 70 years. Pope Callixtus III was so thrilled by the victory of Christian forces that he ordered the bells of every European church to be rung every day at noon, still an existing practice in Hungary. His younger son Mátyás continued his legacy two years after János Hunyadi's untimely death from the plague, which he contracted at Belgrade.

Mátyás' thirty-two-year long reign (1458-1490) is considered by Hungarians to be the country's golden age, and Mátyás himself is the most popular historical figure, as recent polls have revealed. His cult is based on the legends and tales of Hungarian folklore and persistently reinforced even by such popular cultural products as a cartoon series based on tales about the king's good deeds when he mingled among the people in disguise. Some of these are even available in English on YouTube (e.g. King Mathias' tale - There Was Only Once a Dog Market at Buda). His benevolent figure, who rewards the good and punishes the bad, is dear to Hungarian hearts, adults and children alike. However, it is always a risky enterprise to write about this great Renaissance king because of the myths surrounding his life and actual deeds.

The real story of his reign is much more prosaic. One thing is certain, in his lifetime he was not popular either among the ruling elite of barons, nor among his people. Though he was an elected king due to a compromise between rival factions of barons, they were condescending about his low origins. On the other hand, the people who were so nostalgic about his rule after his death surely were not happy to pay the new taxes he levied amounting to a 400% increase to finance the wars conducted by his standing army.

The clue to this paradox is that Mátyás was raised to power at a time of feudal disorder, when a strong central government was in demand. Due to his early education, he embodied all the qualities conducted by great humanists of the time. He had vision and ambition, accompanied by erudite knowledge, tactfulness and perseverance. He envisaged a strong Hungary and aspired to acquire the title of Holy Roman Emperor to counter-balance the threatening advance of the Ottoman Empire. This explains the numerous wars he conducted against the Czech and Austrian provinces. At the same time his huge Black Army secured the southern borders of the country against the Turks. His centralizing efforts included financial and administrative reforms which stabilized the country and brought prosperity not only in the economy but in the arts as well. His sumptuous court at Buda and Visegrád welcomed Italian artists, men of letters and scientists. His famous library Bibliotheca Corviniana contained about 3000 fine codices, including the works of mainly Greek and Latin authors. His fascination for the Italian Renaissance might explain his generous patronage of the arts and his choosing to marry Beatrice, the daughter of the King of Naples in 1476.

Mátyás died unexpectedly in Vienna in 1490, the city he captured from his Habsburg rival Frederick III only five years earlier. His death left the country in disarray, since his designated heir, John Corvinus, his only child but illegitimate, was not accepted by the Hungarian nobility as their king. His lifetime achievement of a strong Hungary vanished into feudal turmoil again. Not only justice died with Mátyás, as the popular saying goes, but his empire as well. He remains the last national king since afterwards only foreign rulers reigned and the gap between the development of Hungary and Western Europe widened for centuries to come, due to a 150-year long Turkish rule, then an even longer Habsburg rule until 1918. Never again did Hungary win a war, and never did it have a ruler to match Mátyás's qualities, which might be an explanation of the belief in all the myths surrounding his character.

As far as the dispute over his ethnic affiliation is concerned, a rare happy ending occurred in 2011 when, after a joint effort by the Hungarian and Romanian governments, Mátyás'renovated statue in Kolozsvár was unveiled to the joy of both nations.

István Széchenyi, The Greatest of the Magyars

Left: Count István Széchenyi
Right: Széchenyi on the 5000 Hungarian forint banknote

Széchenyi offers one year's income of his estate to establish and endow the Hungarian Academy of Sciences

Whose sad eyes gaze at you from the 5000-forint banknote? Whose idea was it to connect Buda and Pest by a chain bridge and merge the twin cities? Whose idea was it to set up an Academy of Sciences to safeguard the Hungarian language and cultivate young minds because –as he said – only an educated nation can create prosperity. Thus, Széchenyi, became the forerunner of what in EU jargon we call, a knowledge-based society.

István Széchenyi was born in 1791 into one of the most respected Hungarian aristocratic families. The Széchenyis excelled in their devotion to the advancement of the country; out of their ranks there was even an archbishop, or just take Ferenc Széchenyi, his father, who founded the National Museum in 1823.

With this background he was destined to serve the country to his best. However, the path to deserving the epithet the 'greatest Hungarian' which Lajos Kossuth, his ardent political opponent, stuck on him in 1830 in a speech to the deputies, was long and tedious.

His reputation as a fearless hussar cavalry officer was established in the Napoleonic wars and he lived the life of a celebrated hero, the favourite of Viennese salons, a boozer and seducer of young hearts. Széchenyi's unbridled temperament and passionate character is to be blamed for his falling in love with his elder bother's wife. The breakdown he suffered due to her unexpected death in 1820 diverted him to another great passion: assuming leadership in modernizing his homeland.

After 17 years of military career he submitted to his father's will and entered the political arena. His debut occurred in

1825 at the Reform Diet in Pozsony (Bratislava today) where he shocked his audience by speaking Hungarian instead of Latin, and by offering one year's revenue from his estates to establish a scientific society (the predecessor of the Academy of Sciences) to nurture the language.

Hungary in the 1820s was an exotic land (a pretty euphemism for backwardness), as Metternich's famous bon mot "Asia begins at the Landstrasse" described the civilizational divide between Austria and Hungary. The *crème de la crème* of the Hungarian aristocracy spent most of its time and money in Vienna while the rest of the country lived in a dumb feudal idyll. However, the early nineteenth century saw the first signs of national awakening culminating in what later was called the Reform Era, including legislative reforms and language reform to make the Hungarian language apt for science and modernity.

This was the point where Széchenyi broke in, stirring up the lukewarm complacency of his countrymen. Driven by the vision of emancipating Hungarians to a European level, he advocated economic renewal by implementing technological innovations like railways, steam navigation, modern estate management, horse-breeding, etc. He travelled widely all over Europe but wherever he went was a study tour for him. With a keen eye he picked the thing that could be beneficial for his country. A good example of this attitude was his visit to France for the coronation of Charles X where instead of the ceremonies the Canal du Midi grabbed his attention, an idea that he later utilised for the regulation of the two main rivers of Hungary, the Danube and the Tisza.

Széchenyi's missionary zeal made him confront all those who opposed his reforms. His provocative, though epoch making book Hitel (Credit), in which he formulated his vision for the modernization of the country, divided the ruling class and alienated the Habsburgs – who saw only the rebel in him, as –again – Metternich told him in a private audience: "You are the greatest threat to the Monarchy."

The 1830s were his most prosperous years, when he was adored by the public, succeeding in carrying out grandiose projects like making the Danube navigable down to the Black Sea or starting his pet project, the first permanent bridge connecting Pest and Buda. His final aim was to make a unified Budapest the new Centre. It was also in this decade, in 1836, that he married the widow Countess Cresencia Seilern after eleven years of secret love.

The 1840s, however, brought his political and personal downfall. The seeds he sowed grew wild plants, to put it metaphorically. His radical rival, Lajos Kossuth, and the younger generation meant a threat to all his achievements by demanding independence (from the Austrian point of view secession). The Revolution that broke out on March 15, 1848 and the war of independence that followed shook him so much that in September 1848 he collapsed mentally and was hospitalized in Döbling, near Vienna, where he stayed for the remaining twelve years of his life.

His tragedy can be seen as a mirror picture of the tragedy of the nation he built. He was full of self-incrimination, blaming himself for the course of events, saying "I started it." In the asylum he regained his mental power and with his pen he continued to be a threat to the suppressing regime of Franz Joseph, whom he considered a usurper. After repeated harassment by the Austrian secret police due to his satirical pamphlet *Ein Blick* his shot body was found with a revolver lying on his left leg on April 8, 1860.

Very rarely in history does posterity seem to be grateful. The beautiful and prophetic words of the poet János Arany - "Never dies he who spends the fruit of his prosperous life on millions..." - proved to have come true when in the 2007 polls asking who was the greatest Hungarian people put him at number one.

Albert Apponyi, The Architect of Trianon

Left: Photo of Apponyi Albert (1900)
Right: Portrait of Apponyi Albert (1910)

Apponyi in Paris for the Treaty of Trianon; 1920

My birthday has been stolen. June 4th ceased to be a day of joy and gaiety ten years ago when it was declared a "national mourning day", which was recently softened to "the day of national unity." It's all because of the coincidence with the anniversary of signing the Treaty of Trianon on June 4, 1920 concluding Hungarian defeat in World War I. Since then the name of this palace in Versailles has become a synonym of national tragedy matchable only with Mohács, a city in Southern Hungary where the Hungarians lost to the Turks in 1526.

Public opinion holds that the man who negotiated the peace treaty was Count Albert Apponyi. Actually, he hardly ever negotiated with the victors, neither did he sign the treaty. His role as the head of the Hungarian Delegation was downgraded to being given an opportunity to address the Allies at Quay d'Orsay on 16 January after he was handed the dictates of the peace treaty. Clemenceau, Lloyd George and the rest listened patiently to his one-hour speech (in French, English and Italian), a rhetorical masterpiece. Opinions about the speech are as diverse as attitudes towards Trianon. It was an apology for the historical merits of Hungary, arguing in favour of keeping the Kingdom of Hungary intact and warning against delegating powers of state building to "culturally inferior" peoples like the Slovaks, Romanians, etc. No wonder it made little impact on the Great Powers whose interests were just the contrary. The only sympathetic reaction came from the British Prime Minister, who inquired about the three million Hungarians who found themselves in a new country overnight as a result of truncating Hungary's territory to a third of its size.

Apponyi, of course, cannot be held responsible for the national trauma Trianon caused, but since he was an authentic representative of the "historical ruling class," part of the blame for the humiliation of the country in 1920 should be put on him as well. His brain child was the 'Lex Apponyi' that became effective in 1907 when as a minister of culture he ordered Hungarian to be the quasi official language in schools, thus enforcing 'magyarization' in a multicultural kingdom at a time when all these nationalities craved for emancipation. The paradox is that he did it out of good convictions, with a deep belief in the civilizing mission of Hungarians in the Carpathian basin.

The Apponyis were one of the oldest aristocratic families in Hungary, conservative and devoutly pro-Habsburg. Born in 1846, Albert Apponyi was destined to go into politics. It ran in the family. His father, who was the Hungarian Chancellor in Vienna, brought him up to be a good Hungarian. His orator's voice and debating skills combined with an impeccable moral stature made him more than a politician, rather an outstanding statesman in his long parliamentary career which started at the age of 26 and lasted until the end of his life. Most of the time he was the leading figure of the opposition in an era when the political divide lay between the pro-monarchy compromise seekers and the advocates of Hungarian independence. He liked to label himself as a Hungarian Tory in the best sense of the word. However, his role as the propagator of Hungarian cultural hegemony at the turn of the century turned out to be a cul-de-sac as this intolerant political course led to the break-up of the Monarchy. Even after the Trianon Treaty was concluded he was adamant in his stubborn stand for the revision of the

Treaty as the Hungarian representative at the League of Nations until his death at the age of 87.

In a sense he remains a tragic figure of Hungarian history. He devoted his life to serving the nation even at the expense of getting married at the age of 50, but due to false doctrines like cultural supremacy and a lack of understanding realities at a time when it was essential to choose appropriate alliances, he seems to have failed in serving the interests of the nation to its best.

The celebrated statesman, the advocate of the nation, the Grand Old Man of Central Europe was given a state funeral in Budapest following his unexpected death in Geneva in 1933, where his duty was to make a speech at the League of Nations. But then, we are all stuck with the legacy. Especially, the Trianon metaphor, the historical wound. It's still an open wound with seemingly no remedy due to insane intolerance from all sides concerned. Hungarians still suffer from the trauma of the truncation of Greater Hungary and cherish a dream when all Hungarians can unite in brotherhood while the Slovaks, the Romanians and others keep referring to Hungarian arrogance. Fortunately, this never-ending cultural war continues dominantly at the political level. People in mixed nationality villages and cities don't give a damn about it. Or, at least let's hope so.

Mihály Károlyi, The Red Count

Left: Photo of Mihály Károlyi (1923)
Right: Statue of Mihály Károlyi at the Kossuth Square in Budapest; removed in 2009 and-re-erected 2012 in Siofok

Mihály Károlyi was elected first President of the Republic of Hungary

Go and take a photo of the statue of Károlyi next to the Parliament building before its removal, recently initiated by a leading figure of the ruling government. [1]A masterpiece by the sculptor Imre Varga erected in 1975, it displays an old man with stature bending slightly over his stick. Late October is the season when the statue is daubed with red paint or defiled by a written note saying "traitor" or "I am responsible for Trianon" put there by anonymous but definitely ultranationalist hands, only to be followed by demonstrations by the liberal and left-wing camps.

What generates such passionate, even hysterical outbursts concerning the first President of the Republic of Hungary which was proclaimed over the ruins of the dissolved Austro-Hungarian Monarchy on 31 October 1918?

Unlike many respectable statesmen and nation-builders of Hungary, he was not considered a serious politician but came in handy as a scapegoat for the failures following World War I. As a politician he would have passed unnoticed in history as the leader of a tiny pacifist party, had not circumstances propelled him accidentally to the forefront of politics in 1918. The less than five months he spent as the head of the newly formed Hungary in the wake of the Aster Revolution is considered one of the tragic periods of Hungarian history in spite of his having

---

[1] In 2012, during the renovation of the Kossuth Square, Károlyi's statue was moved to Siófok. At the same time throughout Hungary, many cities changed streets names which were named after Mihály Károlyi. In Budapest for example the prominent street "Károlyi Mihály utca" in downtown, was changed to simply "Károlyi utca", removing the association with him.

introduced numerous long over-due radical social reforms and universal suffrage.

What caused the failure of his regime was his inability to preserve the territorial integrity of the country. In spite of his entente sympathies he failed to negotiate a decent armistice in Belgrade with Marshal Louis d'Esperey of France. His negotiating position was surely not strengthened by having a Minister of Defence in his first cabinet who -uniquely for someone in his position- proclaimed "I want to see no more soldiers" and who, taking a defeatist stand, practically disbanded the Hungarian armed forces. Having been put under further pressure from idealised entente friends to cede further Hungarian territories he transferred all power to the Social Democrats on March 21 1919, who then fused with the Communists, leading to the formation of the 133-day long Hungarian Communist Republic of 1919 under the leadership of Béla Kun. Though he later denied signing the proclamation that transferred power, it is still the act for which he is blamed for being a traitor.

Putting aside the unfortunate political role he played, he is a most engaging though controversial character. Born in 1875 into one of the most powerful historical aristocratic families, he had every opportunity. The Károlyis, though traditionally ardent pro-Habsburgs, were famed for undertaking social responsibility, especially Mihály's uncle Count Sándor Károlyi, whose fortune he inherited in 1906 after the uncle's death. Mihály Károlyi's flirtation with leftist, later in his life even communist, ideas was perhaps a compensation for his speech defect, but perhaps more due to self-hatred of his own class. The major paradox, which applies also to his wife, the Red Countess, Katinka Andrássy, is that he advocated democracy verbally, and even determined on giving up his inherited wealth to the masses, but when it came to practicalities he proved to be naïve and innocent, a dilettante and a dreamer, in other words everything a serious politician should not be. No wonder the title of his memoirs is *Faith without Illusion*. To be fair, in the arguments between Károlyi sympathisers and Károlyi detractors we should accept that the belief he had in communism was sincere, but illusions were still there. The latter is supported by his later role as an emigré when until the late 1930s he was an uncritical supporter of Stalin's Soviet Union, and later in 1947 he was gullible enough to accept an official position from Rákosi to be the Hungarian ambassador in Paris only to resign when the Rajk show-trials started two years later.

His death in Vence, France in 1955 was publicised in Rákosi's Hungary in a one-sentence note at the back of the official party daily newspaper. At the initiative of his wife Mihály Károlyi was reburied in Budapest during the post 1956 Revolution regime seven years later, an event used by the Kádár regime to make him a cult figure.

And there he still stands steadfast next to the Parliament on the exact spot where the statue of Prime Minister István Tisza, his main political opponent during World War I, used to stand until it was demolished in 1945. The red paint may come and go, the nationalists may cry traitor, the liberals may come to his defence to claim what a real democrat he was, but what remains is the weary look of an old man who became the victim of unhealed wounds from Hungarian history.

Anna Kéthly, A Friend of Social Justice, a Thorn in the Side of Politicians

Left: Bronze statue on marble base by Benedek Nagy (2015) -
Széchenyi rakpart, Budapest
Right: The statue of Anna Kéthly in Budapest, Kéthly Anna Square

Commemorative plaque of Anna Kéthly in Distr. XIII, Pozsonyi u.
40, Budapest

Wayfarers! The best Hungarian Who's Who lies at your feet: it is not a dictionary, but the street names that surround you while you walk. For the past twenty years, Hungarians have had to relearn many street names following the changes of the democratic transition (several hundreds of street names were altered in Budapest). This may seem peculiar, but it is nothing new. Shifting power regimes were obsessed with demonstrating their ideologies by renaming streets and institutions. For example, 'Oktogon' was called 'Mussolini Square' between 1936 and 1945, was renamed 'November 7 Square' to commemorate the anniversary of the October Revolution in Russia (dated to 7 November 1917 in the Gregorian Calendar), and then renamed as 'Oktogon' again in 1990.

One refreshing exception is a tiny square in Erzsébetváros called Anna Kéthly tér. It was formed by demolishing two dilapidated blocks and named after one of the most charismatic figures of the Hungarian Social Democratic Party in 2005. No street or institution could have been named after her under any previous regime, as her uncompromising character made her a thorn in the side of most political powers.

Born and raised in a working class family, her political career began with membership in the Social Democratic Party in 1917 at the age of 28. Her fine rhetoric and erudition assisted her greatly in becoming an MP in 1922, a post she kept until 1948, regardless of changes in government. Her agenda in the rightist, post-feudal political regime before World War II focused on social justice and workers' rights. The liberation of the country from fascism in 1945 drove her to believe that her elusive political ideal,

47

socialism under a democratic system, was an achievable goal. However, the work of the small, but arrogant communist party led by Stalin's best pupil, Mátyás Rákosi, crushed her dreams in 1948. As an ardent defender of democratic values, she opposed the forced fusion of her party, and as a result she was not only expelled by the communist-leaning leftists in the SPD, but soon put under house arrest. In 1950 she was sentenced to life in a show trial against social democrats. She was released only four years later under international pressure. Her vigour and commitment to the social democratic cause, however, was not broken. When asked about her time in prison she said "it was not any worse for me than for the others."

Her unrelenting fight against authoritarianism landed her in Imre Nagy's coalition government during the 1956 revolution as a State Minister and leader of the reorganized SDP. This role was to influence the course of her life. Just before the Russian invasion on November 4 she travelled to Vienna to consult the leaders of the Socialist International, not suspecting that she would never return home afterwards. As the only legitimate representative of the Nagy government abroad, she represented Hungary at the United Nations and helped the world to learn the truth about the '56 revolution and the War of Independence, as the event is officially called these days.

Her life in exile was as active as before. She led the émigré Social Democratic Party abroad and never compromised with the Kádár regime, which she considered illegitimate. Though she was wooed to return to Hungary, her reply was: "not before there are no Russian troops stationed in

Hungary and not until there is a multi-party system and free elections held."

She died in Belgium in 1976, and her final wish was to be buried on Hungarian soil. Her request was granted only 16 years later when she was re-buried in the cemetery where other victims of the post-1956 terror regime lie.

No wonder she despised the political elite of the Kádár regime who she disdainfully called "people of the minute and paid agents". She was a strong woman of principle with iron determination and a dedication to social justice, a role-model our country should not be tempted to forget.

László Rajk, The Man who was Buried Three Times

Left: László Rajk on International Workers' Day in 1947
Right: László Rajk's tomb at Kerepesi cemetery

Speech at the ceremony of March 15th 1947 at Kossuth Lajos Square, Budapest

If months had colours, November would be black in the Hungarian mind, and not just because of the often miserable weather that follows October's "Old women's summer", as it is called in Hungary. While Halloween is a joyful, noisy fiesta with bright colours and lots of fun in most Anglo-Saxon countries, it is a weird custom for Hungarians, as November 1st is the Day of the Dead in Hungary; and you'd better take it seriously. It's an official holiday when people go on the move to visit and tend their closest relatives' graves and light candles - the illuminated cemeteries on this day provide a truly magical and unique spectacle.

Burial rituals vary from culture to culture, but Hungarians excel at one thing: reburials. It's a special way of giving a proper last tribute to the deceased. It all started in the 19th century when our national heroes who died in exile, such as Kossuth, were brought back to rest in Hungarian soil. According to the moral command of poet Mihály Vörösmarty:

May fortune's hand bless or beat you

Here you must live and die!*

(*Translated by Laszlo Korossy)

In our most recent history, reburials acquired political significance and triggered controversy, popular discontent and even uprising. On June 16th 1989 the collapse of Communism in Hungary was accelerated by the reburial ceremony of Imre Nagy, the martyred Prime Minister of the '56 Revolution. The script of the event resembled László Rajk's rehabilitation and reburial on October 6th 1956, which was followed by the outbreak of the revolution on 23rd October.

For those who were not socialized in this country it must be an impossible task to fathom the significance of these events. I was in the crowd at Hősök tere on June 16th 1989, and perhaps would have felt the same at Rajk's funeral: some sort anger at those still in power, self-recrimination for 'how we could have tolerated all this for so long,' but most of all I felt relief, joy and hope that from now on things would change for the better. The confession of those in power that 1956 was not a counter-revolution (but just the opposite) meant they admitted that nothing else they said was true either. I suppose the 200,000 strong crowd at Rajk's funeral must have felt the same way: the admission that he was sentenced and executed on false charges on October 15th 1949 questioned the legitimacy of the whole regime.

The circumstances that led to Rajk's tragic end reflect all the calamities of 20th century Hungarian history. László Rajk was a charismatic and extremely popular figure of the post-war Hungarian Communist Party. Born in Transylvania in 1909 (then part of Hungary) László was the eleventh of 13 children born into a shoemaker's family. He only came to Budapest at the age of 15 when he followed his brother Endre, who was ten years his senior. László studied to be a teacher (French and philosophy) and soon became involved with the illegal Communist movement. He joined the party in 1931. At the opposite extreme of the political spectrum, his brother Endre became a *Hungarista* ('hungarist'– the Hungarian version of a National Socialist Movement), and he had a shining career as an Undersecretary in charge of food supplies in the puppet fascist government of Ferenc Szálasi. In contrast, after being arrested for involvement in organizing the construction workers' strike, László had to leave Hungary in 1935, and he fought in the Spanish Civil War in the 13th International Brigade. Six years later he returned illegally, and became the Secretary of the still illegal Communist Party. For this he was arrested in 1944 and escaped death only through the intervention of his fascist brother. Despite the ideological rift between the two brothers, their kinship proved stronger: when Endre was interned by the Allies in 1945, László returned the gesture, and saved Endre's life by deleting his name from the repatriation lists.

Rajk's active political career was short but most effective. He became the Communist Minister of the Interior in March 1946 and was the main architect of the build up to the complete Communist takeover of the country. His fanatical belief in the Communist cause is to be blamed for his involvement in setting up the ÁVH, the dreaded secret police organization of the time. However, his blind faith caused his ultimate downfall as well, and in May 1949 he was arrested on false charges. Following an Orwellian show trial, he was executed four months later by his fellow Communists.

This trial served as the theme for Péter Bacsó's cult film "A Tanú" (The Witness), where the figure of Daniel is based on Rajk. The black humour of the film contributed much to our remembering Rajk as the victim of a diabolically absurd regime.

The saga of the Rajks is typical of the turmoil of Hungarian history. László's controversial legacy is a lesson to be learnt from. Though he received justice in 1956, his son, László Rajk junior, who at the time of his father's arrest was only four months old, allotted him a third burial, taking his ashes as far away as possible from the grave of János Kádár, who was the chief culprit in forcing Rajk to succumb to the false charges in the name of the party and the cause.

Voices

Mihály Vörösmarty, The Voice of Despair and Hope

Left: Portrait of Mihály Vörösmarty (1857)
Right: Bust of Mihály Vörösmarty in Bonyhád (by Szabó György, 1990)

Statue on Vörösmarty tér in Budapest. Sculptors: Ede Kallós and Ede Telcs (1908)

It was 1842 when forty-two year old Mihály Vörösmarty, celebrated national poet, set off towards a literary café called "Csiga" in order to escape the drudgery of his own home. An auctioneer had just sold his furniture to help relieve a debt owed to a printer. After shelling out to have one of his books published, Vörösmarty had only managed to sell twenty copies: the great poet's patriotic zeal must have numbed his sense of profit. Perhaps it was luck, but he bumped into the illustrious Lajos Kossuth on the way, who became so infuriated by his admired poet's misfortune, that he wrote an article about it in the daily paper he edited. Fulminating about "shame and scandal", he reprehended his readership for their apathy towards the patriotic cause. In a week all of the books were sold.

Coming from an impoverished lesser noble family, Vörösmarty had acquired fame through his national epic, "The Flight of Zalán" twenty years earlier, and by 1830 he was among the few paid members of the newly founded Academy of Science. By 1842, when the aforementioned incident took place, he was regarded as a leading figure amongst the intellectuals and patriots who were shaping Hungarian nationhood.

His private life contained no extraordinary adventures: as a young man he made a living by working as a private tutor for the three sons of the wealthy Perczel family (he also harboured an undeclared love for their sister). In the meantime he studied law (a typical career path for children of resourceless nobility), supported his widowed mother, and generally struggled to make ends meet. He became a loyal follower of Kossuth, and in spite of his cautious aversion to revolution, he took office in the revolutionary government, and went into hiding after its collapse in 1849. After a few months he gave himself up, and was cleared by the occupying authorities. However, he never regained his peace of mind, and his life ended in mental disarray.

Still, it is Vörösmarty's character that makes him an exciting person. His puritanical way of life and lack of means destined him to become a man of letters, and he was thus swept up in the whirlwind of ideas and thoughts that became what we now call the Age of Reform, the great era of Hungarian national revival from the 1820s to 40s. The stakes were to modernize a fossilized feudal society or remain a Germanised, backwater colony in the Habsburg Empire. Intellectuals of the day were much influenced by the prophecy of Herder, a German philosopher, who explicitly stated that small people like Hungarians would simply quit the stage of history. This vision of "the death of the nation" has haunted Hungarians ever since. It was Vörösmarty who first poeticized this morbid thought in the twelfth stanza of his *Szózat* ("Appeal"):

Around the graves where we shall die

a weeping world will come

and millions will in pity gaze

upon the martyrs' tomb.

(trans. Kirkconell, Watson)

The 'Appeal' (1836) has become the credo of all Hungarians, and it contains a maxim that is imprinted on every Hungarian soul: be loyal to your homeland, as (whether you like it or not), it is here that you are destined to live - and die. The poet appeals to his countrymen to make a pledge of allegiance to Hungary in the fear that the nation would otherwise perish:

> *Oh, Magyar, keep immovably*
>
> *your native country's trust,*
>
> *for it has borne you, and at death*
>
> *will consecrate your dust!*

His other major admonition which moves Hungarians émigrés to tears is:

> *No other spot in all the world*
>
> *can touch your heart as home –*
>
> *let fortune bless or fortune curse,*
>
> *from hence you shall not roam!*

The effect of the 'Appeal' lasts even today. School celebrations and official festivities start with Kölcsey's solemn anthem (God bless the Hungarian...), but end with the 'Szózat', and some Hungarian television channels finish at night with a powerful chorus singing the 'Appeal'. Even if Vörösmarty had not written another line of poetry, he would still be considered as one of the greatest Hungarian poets.

His literary oeuvre includes a popular fairy play called *Csongor és Tünde* (most probably inspired by Midsummer Night's Dream), a number of philosophical and love poems (inspired by his great love, Laura Csajági, who was 25 years his junior when he married her in 1843), and his swan-song, "The Old Gypsy", which was written a year before his tragic death. It is a forceful monologue from a mind tortured by the losses the nation had to suffer, but ending with a crescendo of bright light representing hope in the future: "There'll be again a feast-day on this earth." (trans. Dixon, Alan).

His grand funeral in 1855 became a silent protest against the oppressive regime of the Habsburgs, and set a precedent for a long line of funerals and reburials of national heroes (such as Lajos Kossuth in 1896, Ferenc Rákóczi in 1903, László Rajk in 1956, and Imre Nagy in 1989). The political overtones of these reburials signalled a form of non-violent protest.

A larger than life statue composition, erected in 1908, stands at the square named after him. His seated figure, in the pose of a thinker who keeps a watchful eye over the figures of everyday people who surround him, symbolizes best what he stands for in Hungarian culture. It's still a mystery to me what the people on the nearby Gerbeaud terrace, mainly tourists these days, make of this sculpture. But then they never grew up singing the "Szózat", and thus, surely, they fail to recognize its echo.

Franz Liszt, A Lover of Music and Women

Left: Earliest known photograph of Liszt (1843)
Right: Liszt in March 1886, four months before his death,
photographed by Nadar

Liszt giving a concert for Emperor Franz Joseph I (before 1890)

Liszt spent a considerable amount of his life on the roads of Europe touring from Paris to St Petersburg, from Vienna and Pest to as far as Istanbul mainly in a luxury coach designed especially for him, and carrying a Hungarian passport. However, the great Hungarian patriot of whom we are so proud of could not get Hungarian citizenship these days according to the present Hungarian immigration law. He was bilingual, spoke and wrote in German and French but never learnt Hungarian properly. At the age of 62 in 1873 he wrote in a letter to a friend: "Despite my lamentable ignorance of the language, I must be permitted to remain from birth to death, in heart and soul a Hungarian, and hence I am anxious to promote the cause of Hungarian music."

His attachment to Hungary was unquestionable though he spent only a limited period of his life in his homeland. His first demonstrative gesture to prove his dedication to the country was in 1838 to help the victims of the Danube floods by organizing a charity concert tour beginning in Vienna, then moving on to Pest. More than thirty years later the Hungarian Parliament passed the Bill to set up the Hungarian Academy of Music whose first president was Liszt Ferenc. Liszt researchers tend to keep up the issue of ethnic affiliation but as my friend Paul Merrick, a dedicated scholar on Liszt - who chose Hungary as his second home - would put it: "He is Liszt Ferenc for the Hungarians and Franz Liszt for the rest of the world. Full stop."

He was born in 1811 in Doborján (Raiding, now in Austria) near Sopron to an Austrian mother and to Adam Liszt, an estate clerk in the services of the Eszterházy family. Liszt's early career and fame was due mainly to his father's PR skills. His son was only six when he discovered his exceptional musical talent and devoted the rest of his short life to promote his son to become one of the most celebrated artists in 19th century Europe. Liszt's 'wunderkind' period lasted from his debut in Sopron when he was nine, followed by studies and further concerts in Vienna and Paris until his father's sudden death in 1827.

After a period of adolescent self-doubt and contemplation he soon reached maturity culminating in his stormy and lasting love affair with the Countess Marie d'Agoult in 1833, who sacrificed her marriage and eloped with Liszt to start an eleven-year relationship the product of which was Liszt's most creative period and three children, Blandine, Cosima (better known as Wagner's wife) and Daniel.

He was a genius and perfectionist in every sense of the word. As a virtuoso pianist, he mesmerized his audience by his technical and performing skills. As a composer he was most innovative and prolific. He was a supporter of programme music and thus influential on 20th century musical trends. His composing period started in Weimar where he settled for more than a decade after the Grand Duchess appointed him Kapellmeister in 1847.

As a conductor he also brought innovative elements into the art. In Weimar he staged 29 operas and conducted 47. It was also in this period when he developed a close relationship with Wagner and assisted with his career.

As a teacher he was most influential, his pupils included, Hans von Bülow (his daughter Cosima's first husband). Liszt was also reputed as a philanthropist. He helped many causes and donated his performing fees lavishly to the

Beethoven monument in Bonn, the Hungarian National School of Music and the building fund of Cologne Cathedral, just to name a few.

Though Queen Victoria presented Liszt with her own bust after he gave a private concert for the Queen in 1886, he was far from Victorian in his sexual mores. The dames of Europe lay at his feet. As young as 17 he fell in love with a (lady of his own age) but her father strictly forbade the blossoming of this promising relationship due to mésalliance. His affairs were legendary though he was committed seriously to only two women, the Countess Marie d'Agoult and Princess Carolyne zu Sayn-Wittgenstein whom he never married, a most unorthodox attitude by the moral norms of the time. The latter entered his life for good in 1847 when Liszt played in Kiev and she followed him to Weimar and later Rome where he took minor orders in the Church after the death of his two children in the 1860s. He had previously become a 'confrater' of the Franciscan order at Pest in 1858.

His late years were spent by living a threefold life travelling between Rome, Weimar and Pest. He died of pneumonia in Bayreuth in 1886, at the age of 74. His colossal monument is a pilgrimage site for music lovers of all nationalities.

Tivadar Csontváry, The Painter of Loneliness

Left: Self-portrait, circa 1896
Right: Tomb of Tivadar Csontváry in Budapest, Kerepesi
Cemetery: 34/2-1-14

The Lonely Cedar, 1907, Csontváry Museum, Pécs

No one has tried harder to go and see the cedars of Lebanon than me. Csontváry's *Solitary Cedar* was so imprinted on my mind that I longed for years to see the real ones and have experienced the painter's inspiration. My craving turned into obstinate determination when my first attempt to cross the Syrian-Lebanese border fell through since it was closed due to some sectarian skirmishes instigated by the Hezbollah. A year later I finally made it to the cedar grove where presumably Csontváry painted his cedar canvases in 1907 (at least according to the plaque placed by the Hungarian Embassy in Lebanon). Having caught sight of the cedars my high expectations were abruptly crushed. They were just trees, ordinary trees whose beauty equals the common acacia on the Hungarian Plain.

Only after reading Csontváry's 20-page autobiography, a most enjoyable read studied extensively by psychopathologists, did I realise where I went wrong: I lacked the divine vision he possessed.

Tivadar Csontváry Kosztka (originally Mihály Tivadar Kosztka), born in Kisszeben (now Sabinov, Slovakia) was a Hungarian painter. He died in 1919 at the age of 72, and during his life painted more than a hundred canvases over 16 years.

Contrary to most artists, painting for him was a divine mission for which he prepared for 14 years by opening a pharmacy and collecting enough capital to devote his life to fulfilling the mission to which he was ordained by some supernatural power.

It all started on 13 October 1880, on a warm "Indian summer"' day when sitting outside his pharmacy at Gács (now Haličský zámok in Slovakia) to take a rest, God spoke to him. Except for one word, the call he heard was in Hungarian, and the voice said: "You will be the greatest ...(?) painter in the world, greater than Raphael." Taking this call absolutely seriously he rushed to Rome the next year to find out why Raphael? Having studied the paintings of the Renaissance genius in the galleries of the Vatican he was relieved to learn why his destiny was to supersede Raphael's art. He concluded briefly that Raphael's paintings simply lacked the divine spirit and did not reflect vital nature. This visit might have given him the clue to his call's missing word, namely "sun path" (naput), a concept he became obsessed with. The divine spirit shows itself in the path of light radiating from the sun, so he interpreted the message.

After leaving his pharmacy behind at the age 41 he set off to Munich to begin his painting career, or rather it should be said "fulfilling his mission." It took him more than a decade of several trips to the Middle East (including Egypt, Palestine, Syria) in search of the Great Motif to unfold the secret of the sun path. He found it in Cairo in 1904 (The Cairo Railway Station at Sunset Lit by Electricity) and it was the light still present when the sun is no longer seen, that is before sunrise and after sunset. This discovery became the credo of his "plein-air" art and that's how he became one of the greatest artists of colour and light, culminating in his magnificent canvas Baalbeck painted in 1906. Only four years and the cedar paintings later he concluded that he had fulfilled his divine mission in this world, and stopped painting.

Like his cedar in faraway Lebanon, he himself became a solitary figure of Pest bohemian life and for the rest of his life was widely mocked for his eccentric political views and vegan diet. His psychosis took over him very intensively and he died in obscurity in Buda's János Hospital leaving his unappreciated canvases in his deserted flat.

It's a mere coincidence of events that we know about him at all and can see most of his works a museum in Pécs that is named after him. A few days after his death his relatives were planning to auction off his canvases to carters to protect their carts when Gedeon Gerlóczy, a young architect with a keen eye for art, decided to invest all his money in purchasing the canvases at the last moment, thus saving most of the "mad artist's" works for posterity. Ten years passed before Csontváry had an exhibition and thirty more before finally he won recognition in Hungary in the midst of controversial critical appraisal. His prophecy that appreciation can only come when you have survived all your contemporaries could not have been truer in his case.

Should you have the opportunity to look at his paintings, take your time and look for the lights and shades of colours - even if there is little chance you can afford to do what Picasso did in 1948 when he visited an ad hoc Csontváry exhibition at the Hungarian Embassy in Paris, and asked his hosts to leave him locked in the room for an hour on his own, after which he simply said: "I never realized that apart from me our century had a great artist."

Molnár Ferenc, The Bohemian Hungarian Who Conquered Broadway

Left: Portrait of Ferenc Molnár (1918)
Right: Commemorative plaque on the wall of his primary school by the artist Johanna Götz

Paul Street Boys Sculpture, Budapest, 8th district, inspired by Molnar's novel: "The Paul Street Boys"

Don't tell a taxi driver in Budapest your destination is Rákóczi tér, otherwise you might get a knowing glance, especially if you're a woman. The square where I have been living for more than thirty years is associated with prostitution and though the girls are long gone, the myth is still there. This is part of multicultural Josefstadt (Józsefváros) where the plot of *The Paul Street Boys* takes place. Written in 1907 and translated into more than a dozen languages it's still a juvenile cult novel, especially for Hungarians – several notions in it have become part of everyday vocabulary like *einstand* (taking away property by force), or *nemecsek ernő* (someone's name written without capitalization as a sign of humiliation).

Its author, Ferenc Molnár – born Ferenc Neumann in 1878 – was not the greatest figure of Hungarian literature in the early decades of the last century, but definitely one of the most popular. Hungarians are excessively proud of their literature, however, the world knows little about it. This is partly because of the language barrier but even of those who are translated, very few rise to international fame. Ferenc Molnár is an exception.

His secret lies in being able to serve the 'basic instincts' of the contemporary audience. Though he started as a journalist, continued as a novelist and short-story writer, he acquired fame as a writer of more than forty plays, mainly comedies and light pieces. Most of his plays were immediate hits, and not only in the Pest theatres but in London, Italy and, thanks to an adept agent, New York.

Molnár was a keen observer of middle- and upper-class urban life, the main strengths of his plays being witty dialogue and a polished style. The choice of his themes included mainly issues concerning male-female relationships, jealousy, adultery, love and hate struggles – things that shocked but pleased the audience. And he was very much at home in these matters. The real secret of the success of his plays is that most of them are autobiographical.

He had five women in his life and it's a major understatement to say that all of these affairs or marriages were stormy. What fuelled his inspiration to write was his reckless, often violent and hysterical character. The first woman Molnár fell deeply in love with was Irén Varsányi who played the leading role in several of his early plays. To his misfortune her husband was jealous enough to challenge him to a duel, and as a result, was imprisoned for two weeks in 1911. To make things worse he meddled in a jealousy fight with Endre Ady, the greatest poet of Hungarian literature, over Margit Vészi whose father was the editor-in-chief of the magazine he worked for. Molnár won – which satisfied his vanity and married her in spite of parental opposition. The marriage ended abruptly due to what we call today domestic violence; to put it more bluntly he beat his wife even when she was pregnant. However, the result of the relationship is Molnár's most popular play *Liliom,* later adapted as the Rodgers and Hammerstein musical *Carousel* (1945), in which the main character, Liliom, a carousel attendant falls passionately in love with a maid whom he mistreats, but her devotion is unshaken despite all his violence ('a slap from the beloved that does not hurt').

After a speedy divorce from Margit he found his real match, a femme fatale, Sári Fedák, the most celebrated primadonna of the day. The 11-year sado-masochistic relationship ended in Fedák's insistence on his marrying her and only then would she let him loose to live with the rising actress Lili Darvas, 20 years his junior. The marriage with Lili turned out to be more peaceful, but only because she told him at the beginning that if he dared to hit her she would smash his skull with a heavy brass candle holder, which she grabbed on the spur of the moment.

Molnár's prolific oeuvre is mainly due to the Bohemian lifestyle that intellectuals, especially the ones with money, could afford in pre-World War II Pest and his wealth due to the income his world fame brought him. As soon as he left Hungary in 1939 to start a new chapter in America, his career declined. Once a Hungarian writer becomes an emigrant, he will lose the soil by which he was enriched. The last traumatic experience he went through was to cope with the suicide of Vanda Bartha in 1947, the fifth woman in his life whose story he commemorated in the novel Companion in Exile. He died as a lonely man in New York in 1952.

If Molnár had written nothing else but *The Paul Street Boys* he'd still be part of the Hungarian literary canon. No writer can dream of a better posterity than he has, due to the revitalizing program Józsefváros is going through. Thanks to an enthusiastic team of young people fiction has become reality, the 'grund' of the Paul Street Boys is recreated for the benefit of children of today. Don't miss it, go and see it for yourself (www.agrund.hu).

Robert Capa, A Pacifist and Eye-witness to Five Wars

Note: The work of Robert Capa and of his partner and love Gerda Taro is still under copyright protection in some countries and therefore can not be shown in this book.

Copyright holder is Magnum Photos (which was cofounded by Robert Capa in 1947); on Magnum Photos' webpage many of Capa's and Taro`s photographs can be found and bought.

Left: Gerda Taro (Capa's partner and love) in 1937
Right: Artwork at the birth house of Federico Borrell García; based on Capa's world famous photograph "The Falling Soldier" (the original photograph is still under copyright protection in some countries)

Robert Capa died holding his camera in his left hand minutes after stepping on a landmine. He was finding the right angle to make a perfect shot of retreating French soldiers in the paddy fields at *Thai-Binh*, North Vietnam, on May 24, 1954. He was the first American journalist killed in Vietnam and the Americans claimed him as a war hero. The U.S. Army offered the family a plot for Capa's burial in Arlington National Cemetery, but Julia Friedmann, Capa's mother, turned it down, saying that her son was not a soldier but a pacifist. He is buried in a Quaker cemetery in Amawalk, NY – now together with his mother, his brother Cornell Capa and Richard Whelan, who documented his short but most intense life.

Though his name may not sound all too Magyaresque, Robert Capa could not have forgotten his Hungarian roots even if he had wanted to. Once he reposted to a questioning British general who was reluctant to issue accreditation documents that "it's not my fault that I was born in Hungary". And born he was in Budapest, as Endre Ernő Friedmann, in 1913. It was a typical story of the time – an average non-religious Jewish family, a tailor father whose only luxury was a little gambling after work, a worrying Yiddish mama and two brothers. It turned out quite early on that Cápa ('shark'), which was his nickname at school, had high adrenalin levels, since he tended to attract trouble. After graduating from the prestigious Madách Gimnázium he fraternized with "bad company," getting involved with the leftist avant-garde literary circle of Lajos Kassák. His hotheadedness in participating in anti-government demonstrations lead to his being forced to leave Hungary, only to return twice afterwards.

After a brief stay in Berlin in 1932 (bad timing) he left for Paris, the dream place of all Hungarian intellectuals. Stricken by day-to-day problems of survival it was here, under the influence of his life-long love Gerda Pohorylles, that he decided to be famous. The first step was to find a catchy name and he thus decided to keep his nickname, which resembled the name of Frank Capra, a noted film director, and add Robert to complement his newfound surname. Gerda became Taro. Capa invented himself as a mega-famous American photographer and even if the little trick was soon found out, the quality of his pictures lived up to his self-proclaimed status as a star.

The path to acquire the label of 'the greatest war photographer of all time" began in 1936 in the Spanish Civil War. What brought him world fame was his photograph of a Spanish Republican militiaman collapsing dead, the so-called Falling Soldier. He witnessed and documented four more wars in the following 18 years: the Second Sino-Japanese War, World War II, the 1948 Arab-Israeli War and the First Indochina War. His iconic images of the invasion D-Day (June 6, 1944) and hundreds of other unique photographs left their mark on photojournalism.

Capa set an example for war correspondents that would last into the future by unveiling the senselessness of all wars and working up the "hyena" dilemma of "scavenging" photographers. Very rarely did he take images of generals or politicians. He set his focus on the G.I., and the horror on the faces of children and ordinary people; Capa had a unique talent for recording emotions, especially the pain caused by war. His idea of making good photography was that "you've got to like people and let them feel you do". On the other hand, his professionalism was due to having been able to cope with the "hyena" syndrome. When a bomber pilot returned from an attack covered in blood, he told Capa, "ok photoreporter, is this the kind of picture you were looking for?" It was at this point when he took an ethical stand: no personal emotion, no involvement, just documentation. This often took courage and – as he put it – 'I am a gambler' and he stayed put defenselessly with his camera while others ran into combat.

What mesmerises me about Capa is the compactness of a most intensive and meaningful life. He burnt the candle at both ends, first dedicating himself to documenting reality in a way only few could, then falling into the self-made trap of competing only with himself to be the best. He also had to cope with the burden of being a man without a country. All other pleasures like women (including a brief affair with Ingrid Bergmann), poker and gambling and countless bottles of whisky were just narcotics that helped him fulfill his mission.

The Robert Capa Gold Medal is awarded annually by the Overseas Press Club of America for the "best published photographic reporting from abroad requiring exceptional courage and enterprise".

István Örkény, Chronicler of Absurdity

Left: István Örkény in 1974
Right: István Örkény's One Minute Stories, depicted by guerilla knitters at Örkény István Theater (Budapest)

Örkény István Theater in Budapest (2016)

Over the years, Örkény has caused me much embarrassment. Whenever I tried to explain the complexities of what it means to be Hungarian to my western friends, I often cut it short by recommending that they read István Örkény's *One Minute Stories*. The embarrassment only came afterwards, when they admitted that they could not make much sense of the whole thing. Was this due to Örkény's ironic view of things, his grotesque vision of life, or the absurdity of the situations he described? It seems to me now, that it was probably all of these.

During his long literary career, Örkény developed his own unique approach to describe reality, the fertile soil for which was 20th century Hungary and its history, characterized by political upheavals and constant uncertainty. The literary genre most suited to reflect this was the grotesque, which, in his own words, requests that the reader views the world in the following way: "Please assume a straddle stance, lean far forward, and remain in this position while looking backwards through your legs. " (*The Grotesque* – trans. Gwen Jones). The path that led him to this form of expression was long and arduous: although he was already active in the literary scene by the late 1930s, he only matured into the Örkény of the grotesque as we know him today in the early 1960s.

A western reporter once asked him: "Was it beneficial to your literary work that you were bourgeois, Jewish, communist and Hungarian all in one?" His answer: "Definitely. And it would have even been more useful had I also been black and a leper." To this, the reporter could have added that he was also a P.O.W., a "silenced" writer, or a full-time employee of the Nutriment Factory. All these biographical details are true.

He was born in 1912 into a well-established pharmaceutical family who had already Hungarianized their name from Öszterreicher into Örkény, and he was expected to continue the family tradition. After failing an exam in thermodynamics, he left technical engineering to study pharmacy, which turned out to be wise decision since he would use his pharmacology degree later on in his life.

His literary ambitions led him into the radical circle of writers centred on the emblematic figure of Attila József, one of the greatest 20th century poets. After Örkény's father was warned by high-standing officials that his son was keeping "bad company" he was sent to London and Paris, only to come back on the last train from Strasbourg after war broke out on Sept 1, 1939.

He was called up to the Hungarian army as a medical officer in 1942 but was stripped of this rank due to his Jewish ancestry, and following the fatal defeat of the 2nd Hungarian Army at Voronezh in 1943, he became a POW. Örkény only arrived home four years later, with the sole ammunition of a few sociographic pieces and a drama which never reached the stage.

After the ordeals of war, he succumbed to the jubilant mood of reconstruction, joined the ranks of Communist writers, and produced reports and novels celebrating the new era. However, Örkény was soon disillusioned by Rákosi's oppressive rule and took a self-critical role in the 1956 Revolution. It was he who formulated the infamous bonmot on the role of radio in the Communist regime: We lied all night, we lied all day, we lied on every wavelength.

He was reluctant to defend the post-56 Kádár regime while his fellow writers were imprisoned for their role in the Revolution, and this led to his silencing, in other words a publication ban, a punitive measure employed against intellectuals who had fallen out of political favour.

While struggling to make a living as a pharmacist at the United Pharmaceutical and Nutriment Factory, he wrote incessantly – "for the desk drawer". It was during this period that he honed his technique of the grotesque: one-minute stories. He wrote some 400 of these philosophical sketches using naked prose to depict the absurdity of everyday insanity, whether it was a Jewish professor lecturing his uneducated German guard on Rilke, or a Budapest devastated by the A-bomb. In the former, the infuriated guard shoots the professor, while in the latter, a note is seen at the ruins of Opera House the day after the bomb was dropped: "The wife of Dr Varsányi offers mouse extermination. Customer to supply own bacon." Örkény's bottom line is that although we are trapped by situations created by history or ourselves, there is always hope: one must always act, even if the decision taken turns out to be the wrong one. The same philosophy also shines through in the two plays *The Tót Family* and *Cat's Play* that brought him world fame.

The ice broke in 1962, and he finally attained long-deserved success on the stage and among readers. His untimely death in 1979 left a hiatus in Hungarian literature. However, since the Hungarian reality that Örkény described so powerfully continues to produce a multitude of absurd situations, the immortality of his oeuvre is secured for generations to come.

Zoltán Kodály, The Music Educator of a Nation

Left: Zoltán Kodály in the 1930s
Right: Zeneakademia (Liszt Academy) Grand Hall, 1942, Zoltán
Kodály in the middle

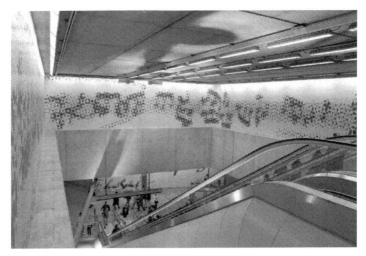

Budapest M4, Kálvin tér station, the decoration on the wall is a
score of Kodály

Andrássy út, the only straight avenue in Pest, is divided into three major sections by two circuses, Oktogon and Kodály körönd . The Körönd, as it was named originally when the four residential blocs surrounding the square were built in the 1890s, fell victim to the re-naming frenzy of the Horthy regime and between 1938 and 1945 was called Adolf Hitler square. Until 1970 it was called just the Körönd (the circus) again and then named after Zoltán Kodály whose 4-room groundfloor flat was there at Andrássy út 89. This turned out to be a good choice since it survived the latest naming/re-naming hysteria of 1990 when more than a thousand street names were changed as a move to erase the Communist past.

Like many great Hungarian artists and historical figures, Kodály devoted his whole life to a single cause: to save the ancient musical heritage of the Magyars and incorporate it into the European style of music. He and his life-long friend Béla Bartók arrived almost at the last moment. Not only did they collect folk songs all over Hungary, they also created a methodology to organize their collection. Their guiding principle during their collecting trips to faraway villages in the first decade of the 20th century was "only from a pure source." They claimed that it's only the folk songs of the peasants that hold real value and pointed to the fact that the oral heritage was kept almost intact for more than two thousand years. Comparative research convinced them of the Asian roots of Hungarian pentatonic music. Their findings were published in the 1930s and comparative ethnomusicology became an accepted discipline.

Kodály was born in Kecskemét in 1882 but due to his father's appointments to various Railway posts he grew up in Galanta (now in Slovakia). His first encounter with music was through his parents and -as he claimed in a speech given to the people of Galanta at a celebration – his nanny and maids from nearby villages who sang him folk songs. He enrolled at the Budapest Pázmány University and the Music Academy in Budapest in 1900. He matured as a composer in the following 20 years but did not acquire fame before 1923 when his major choral work Psalmus Hungaricus was premiered and became an instant success.

He divided his creative energies between composing, teaching and organizing a network to make music available to all, as he said "music is for everyone". His grand plan to make Hungary a nation of music lovers and experts materialized via his idea of introducing music education in all schools at a very early age. Once he summed up his philosophy to his students in his wry manner as follows: this institute (the Music Academy) will remain a college of the deaf and dumb "because anyone who can't write down what he hears is deaf and anyone who can't sing what he sees is dumb."

He subordinated everything to achieve his goal so much so that he accepted several high positions after 1945, including the presidency of the Academy of Sciences. The emerging communist regime flattered him and seemingly intended to use him as an iconic figure to represent the regime. However, Kodály, with his integrity and moral superiority collaborated with the regime only to a degree that served the interests of implementing his desired objective: maintaining Hungarian identity through polishing the Hungarian musical heritage. Due to his international fame and undisputable professionalism he was untouchable so much so that Rákosi's associate Révay, the cultural dictator, had to abandon his idea of having the Hungarian anthem starting with the word 'God' rewritten. Kodály's terse answer to the request was "Why do we need a new anthem? The old one will do."

By the 1960s his great plan was materialized. Generations of Hungarians received quality music education, a choral movement flourished and the Kodály method, based on solfége and group singing, became known and popular in many countries, especially Japan, the US and England, although his bon mot concerning the Kodály method was that 'my only method is that I have no method'.

When he died in 1967 at the age of 85 he was still active and adored by his students and ordinary people alike. He had fulfilled his ambition he set before himself as a young man: to make the world better through music.

His legacy lives on in the concert halls and in the memory of many as affirmed by the fresh flowers and wreaths adorning the plaque on the wall of his Körönd apartment.

Myth-makers

Sisi, Queen of the Hungarians

Left: Elisabeth, Queen of Hungary, Coronation photograph (1867)
Right: Sculpture located in St Matthias Church in Budapest,
Hungary

Coronation of Franz Joseph and Elisabeth as Apostolic King and
Queen of Hungary in Buda (1867)

This book is supposed to be about famous Hungarians who we are proud of, regardless of how well known they are internationally. But then there are "honorary" Hungarians as well. Although Franz Joseph's spouse Elisabeth von Wittelsbach had no Hungarian blood, she still deserves a place in the national pantheon as the Guardian Angel of the Hungarians. Wherever you read "Erzsébet" in a place name, it must be named after "Sisi", as she is otherwise known. In Budapest alone we have Erzsébetváros (7th District), Pesterzsébet, and of course, the Erzsébet Bridge: on the Buda side you'll find a statue of her in a romanticized pose. The myth of her role in appeasing Emperor Franz Joseph is unshakable in the minds of Hungarians. No matter what historians might add, we have always been sentimental towards her, and she is considered as "Patrona Hungariae".

However, my schoolboy knowledge of the saintly empress was shattered by a very good friend of mine, Simon Corrigan, who after publishing two novels decided to write a book about Sisi. He even moved from London to Budapest to research her life. In his book, which he never completed due to his untimely passing, he planned to portray her as a neurotic who suffered from manic depression. After endless discussions and bottles of wine we could never agree on Sisi's real character. These conversations still haunt me. Simon was adamant in proving his point by telling me how she went on six-to-eight hour walks, neglected her children, and lived on cold beef broth just to maintain a slim figure. He even thought her open attachment to the Hungarians was an act inspired by selfishness. Of course he had a point, but he could not fathom what lay behind the Hungarians' adulation of Sisi.

It is true that today's psychiatrists would probably treat her for bipolar depression – with lithium instead of cocaine. But then she had every reason to be depressed. She became Franz Joseph's wife as an unbridled teenager at the age of 16 (the Emperor's mother, Sophie, had originally intended her elder sister Helene Wittelsbach to be his spouse). Sisi was then locked away in the Hofburg under the watchful eye of her mother-in-law and her entourage – torture for a young girl who showed a predilection for manly sports. You'll understand a lot more about the perverted protocol of the Habsburgs if you visit the Hofburg in Vienna, and you'll probably end up sympathizing with Sisi's minor rebellions, like demanding her own bathroom and gymnastics rings. Maybe it was the golden cage of regal misery that caused her psychosomatic illnesses. She balanced the claustrophobia with a maniacal passion for travelling, which provided a good opportunity for escape.

It must have been her yearning for freedom and her defiance of the court that drove her to support the Hungarian cause. She learnt Hungarian, and spent a lot of time in Hungary. She irritated the court by surrounding herself with Magyars, and became a life-long friend of Count Gyula Andrássy, "the handsome hanged man," as he was called after seventy-five exiled leaders were hanged in effigy following the Hungarian Revolution of 1848-49. But times change, and so 18 years later Franz Joseph had a change of heart, and appointed Andrássy as Prime Minister of Hungary. The political compromise or "Ausgleich" of 1867 was of course a turning point in Hungarian history: Franz Joseph was crowned as King, and Elisabeth as Queen of Hungary. The Dual Monarchy was created. From then on

Sisi formed the emotional tie between the rebellious Hungarians and imperial Austria. But Sisi needed the Hungarians as much as they needed her. It was a fortunate quirk of history. A less fortunate coincidence was her encounter with a young anarchist named Luigi Lucheni, who stabbed her in the heart in 1898. His original target, the French Duke d'Orleans, had travelled elsewhere, and so he turned on Elisabeth instead. The Hungarian nation mourned her loss. Even today, you can often see freshly cut flowers by her statue at Erzsébet Bridge.

Simon Corrigan (1964-2006)

Tivadar Herzl, Architect of the Jewish Nation

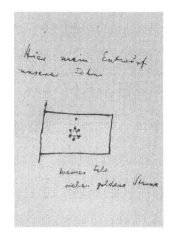

Left: Photograph of Tivadar Herzl (circa 1900)
Right: A sketch in Herzl's diary of a proposed flag for the Zionist movement (1890s)

Honor guard standing next to Herzl's coffin in Israel

On my first visit to Tel Aviv back in the 1980s I went to the Knesset to see Marc Chagall's grandiose frescoes. Once there, I peeped into the Assembly Hall where –to my surprise- the only decoration was a huge portrait of Theodore Herzl behind the Speaker's seat. It was time when diplomatic relations between Hungary and Israel were suspended due to the 1967 war in which the Soviet Union sided with the Arab countries and the rest of the Communist Bloc had to follow suit. Ever since then, Herzl's Moses-like face with sparkling eyes made a deep impression on me.

Though he was born in Pest in 1860, apart from a plaque on the house of his birth next to the Dohány utca Synagogue, there is hardly any trace in Hungary of his cult to resemble the one in Israel, where even a law was passed in 2004 to commemorate his legacy. Indeed, his endowment to the Jewish Cause made history at the time and still polarizes Jews and non-Jews alike.

It all started in the family. Brought up in a secular fashion he received his basic education in the Lutheran Grammar School in Pest. After his sister's death, the family moved to Vienna when he was 18, a fact that later explains his definition of his identity: "I am a German Jew from Hungary." Identity became his topos for the rest of his life. Having a restless mind, even at a young age, Tivadar, was adamant in believing that he was born to fulfill a mission. After studying law and a brief legal career he found his mission in becoming a playwright. Though quite a few of his comedies and dramas were performed in the theatres in Vienna, soon he had to realize that he could not surpass a mediocre level in literature.

Journalism provided much more success, so much so that in 1891 he received an offer from the Neue Freie Presse to be a correspondent for the prestigious Viennese paper in Paris. His Parisian years led him to find the real mission of his life. He became more and more concerned with the issue of anti-semitism sweeping Europe, including the pogroms in Russia, the Dreyfus Trial in 1894, which he attended as a correspondent, and after returning to Vienna in 1895 he found that an arch anti-semite, Karl Lueger - whose famous bon mot was to coin the word 'Judapest' - was elected Mayor.

It was in those days that he had a revelation of what the real solution for the Jewish issue would be. After revising his views on possible ways of assimilating Jews into various European societies, including the option of massive conversion, he came to the conclusion that the only way for the Jews to be free was to have a homeland of their own. The choice for the new home for all Jews fell on Palestine, then under Ottoman rule, though Argentina and later Uganda cropped up as alternatives. But with the solidifying of the idea of rebuilding the City on Mount Zion, Palestine became the only option.

Herzl approached the Rothschilds to support his idea and started to write a detailed argumentation for why the Zionist solution would be the best cure for the plight of the Jews in the poorer part of Europe. Out of this correspondence was born his famous pamphlet, *Der Judenstaadt* (the Jewish State), published in 1896, which led to controversies and heated debates among the Jewish communities, but surprisingly was supported by most anti-semites. *Der Judenstaadt* became the centrepiece of the Zionist Cause, the main point of which was that Jewishness was no longer a social, religious or racial issue, i.e. there was no need for assimilation, but the Jews are a nation who needed to have a state of their own where anti-semitism would vanish and the Jews could take things into their own hands.

Herzl became so agitated by the reaction to his book that he started frantically organizing support for his idea among bankers, politicians and most of all Jewish communities affected by anti-semitism like the Polish, Galician and Russian Jews where he was hailed as a Saviour. Not so much in Hungary, Austria or Germany where Zionism never took roots.

Now that Herzl had written the best script he ever wrote, there was no stopping him from fulfilling a mission he had always dreamed of. Taking his own words literally – 'If you will it, it is not a dream' - he conducted – most of the time fruitless - negotiations with Kaiser Wilhelm II of Germany, Sultan Abdulhamid II, Pope Pius X and innumerable influential statesmen. After visiting Palestine he wrote a novel *Altneuland* (The Old New Land), published in 1902, about the Zionist utopia where in Palestine Jews live freely, convert the desert into fertile soil, democracy flourishes and even the Arabs embrace the newcomers, feeling grateful for their having brought civilization.

In possession of the script for the New State in Palestine, Herzl launched the Zionist movement, the first Congress of which took place in Basle in 1897. There he claimed:

"At Basle I founded the Jewish State. If I said this out loud today, I would be answered with universal laughter. Perhaps in five years, and certainly in fifty, everyone will know it."

What became of the Zionist movement is a different story but the paradox of history is that 50 years later his prophecy came true when, standing beneath his portrait, Ben Gurion proclaimed on May 14, 1948 the formation of Eretz Israel.

Blaha Lujza, The Nation's Nightingale

Left: Portrait of Lujza Blaha (1866)
Right: Photograph of Lujza Blaha (circa 1902)

Photograph from the 25th theater performance of the Grandmother ("A Nagymama") on the 10th of March, 1908 (Lujza Blaha in the middle)

You don't learn much about English or American history when you change buses at Clapham Junction in London or at 43rd Street in Manhattan. However, the whole spectrum of Hungarian history, from the mysterious Chief Örs up to actress Mari Jászai, is revealed as soon as you take the metro, ride tram 6, or just walk the streets of Budapest.

Blaha Lujza tér, at the crossing of the Körút (Ringroad) and Rákóczi út, is the place where "you can change to metro line 2", as you can hear daily over the loudspeaker when you travel on tram 4 or 6. The square (fairly rundown these days, but still a favourite meeting point for many) was named after Blaha Lujza in 1920 when she celebrated her 75th birthday. Her home overlooked the National Theatre, where she was a celebrated primadonna for decades. You can't see the National Theatre (Nemzeti Színház) anymore since it was demolished in 1965 due to the construction of the metro. The farcical saga of building a new Nemzeti then began, only to end in 2001 when an eclectic edifice was erected at the Lágymányosi Bridge.

Blaha Lujza (you can't say Lujza Blaha, we pronounce her name as one word: blahalujza) was special to Hungarian hearts, as she was the 'nightingale of the nation,' a metaphor given to her by writer-poet Mór Jókai, the greatest Hungarian myth-maker. Even Franz Joseph used the term for her when he awarded Blaha Lujza the Imperial Golden Cross in 1900.

Blaha Lujza was born as Ludovika Reindl in 1850 into a family of travelling actors, and her talent for singing soon showed. The close-knit family of troupers just called her 'singing Lujzi', calling her 'little Lujzi' after her mother. The first name stuck to her, unlike her surnames. She had no less than six surnames due to her father's alias, her foster father's name, and the three husbands she had during her lifetime. The only one she always kept was Blaha. It was a sign of respect to Jan Blaha, a Czech conductor in the imperial army, who discovered her talent and educated her. As a special gesture of gratitude for ending the family's misery as itinerant artists, Lujza married him when she was fifteen, only to be widowed five years later. She married two more times.

She made her debut as Kölesi Lujza as a 'sugar baby' at the tender age of fifteen in Szabadka (Subotica, now Serbia), and only six years later she became a member of the National Theatre, which was established in 1830 as part of the national revival. The zenith of her career lasted between 1871 and 1900, when she performed almost 200 parts in theatre plays, called 'Volksstück' in German (vaudeville). This became the dominant genre of popular culture that could arouse national sentiments. The romanticised representation of the Hungarian peasants and celebrations of their simple lifestyle made people feel proud of being Hungarian again. Her immense popularity as a celebrity was due to her singing talent, her charm, and ardent patriotism.

Blaha Lujza also helped popularize a related genre of music. In Mexico you can't escape mariachi bands, in Italy you are raided by street musicians, and the Hungarian version is the Gypsy band, harassing you while eating in traditional restaurants. But their profession seems doomed to extinction in today's era of globalization. One of my greatest fears has always been being approached by the head fiddler who asks what your favourite "nóta" is. I don't have one, even though most self-respecting Magyars do. The chief populariser of these sentimental, melodramatic, syrupy, pseudo-folk songs was in fact Blaha Lujza.

She was much more to Hungarians than a mere singer and actress, as she was the one who gave pride and acceptance to Hungarians in an age when the national spirit still suffered from the trauma of the defeat of the War of Independence, and the division of the nation following the Compromise with the victors in 1867. The formation of the Austrian-Hungarian Dual Monarchy brought economic prosperity and political stability to Hungary for almost half a century. However, German dominance threatened the survival of Hungarian cultural heritage. Blaha Lujza and the like helped to redress the balance.

Her funeral in 1926 attracted a crowd of 100,000, including a 200-member Gypsy band that played the tunes. Her memorial in the Kerepesi Cemetery is one of the finest pieces in the Hungarian national pantheon.

Béla Lugosi, The Resurrection of Count Dracula

Left: Photograph with signature (1912)
Right: Béla Lugosi's star on Hollywood's Walk of Fame

A screenshot from "Dracula"

"Ah, Dracula land." This was how my country was amiably located on the world map at a party in New York back in 1989, after I revealed my nationality. I was bemused but the association of Dracula with Hungarians by foreigners has haunted me ever since.

Though first my ethnic pride was slightly insulted to be linked to Vlad Tepes the Impaler, a 15th century Vlach ruler infamous for his cruelty, and on whose evil character Bram Stoker fabricated the personae of the bloodsucking Count, but I had to admit there was some ground for the link: Transylvania, where Dracula has a cult, used to be part of the Hungarian Kingdom; Hungarian names like Zoltán, the Count's dog, is a typical Hungarian name, but most of all Béla Lugosi, the greatest and most authentic impersonator of the movie Dracula was unmistakably Hungarian with a thick Hungarian accent.

Born as Béla Blaskó in 1882 in Lugos, a small city in south-western Transylvania (now Lugoj, Romania), Lugosi came to world fame at the age of 49 when Tod Browning at Universal Studio hired him with reluctance to play the leading role in the horror movie Dracula. The choice fell to Lugosi mainly because by that time he had played the part more than 500 times on Broadway in a play with the same title. Right after the first night of the film on Valentine's Day 1931 it became a box office hit and shot Lugosi into overnight fame. The secret for the success was not simply the thrilling theme but most of all Béla Lugosi's authenticity and acting power through which he formed the Count's character with a high level of professionalism and empathy.

He was not a newcomer to either stage or cinema. His strict banker father wanted the youngest of his four children to follow his trade but unruly Béla thought otherwise. After encountering a travelling troupe of actors he quickly made up his mind to join them and ran away from home at the age of 12 never to return to Lugos. Lugosi, with his characteristic blunt sense of humour mentioned once with some self-irony: "Every actor is somewhat mad, or else he`d be a plumber or a bookkeeper or a salesman."

After learning the art of acting in various cities he ended up in Budapest and polished his talent so well that in 1912 he was hired by the prestigious National Theatre. He fought and was wounded in WW I, an experience that gave him more ammunition to develop his skills to make the drama and horror of real life perform authentically on stage.

The turning point of his life was when he became politically active in Bela Kun's Council Republic. Little is it known that British and American cinema had been enriched by three outstanding Hungarian artists due to the crush of the short-lived communist regime in 1919, which was followed by the white terror aimed at all those who were instrumental in the 'red' experiment to create a workers' state. Sir Alexander Korda aka Korda Sándor, Michael Curtiz aka Kertész Mihály and Béla Lugosi were politically active in the commissariat of education and culture, the latter organizing the actors' trade union. All three had to leave promptly after the collapse of the regime. Lugosi ended up in the United States a year later where he became a U.S. citizen in 1931, the same year the Dracula movie was made.

Though this would be the role that would keep his name for posterity, he suffered from being stranded in one genre from which he felt he could never break out. In his own words: "It's a living, but it's also a curse. It's Dracula's curse.

... I'd like to quit the supernatural roles and play just an interesting, down-to-earth person." He never managed, although he played in more than 160 movies including Frankenstein with his partner Boris Karloff.

The major crisis in his life and career occurred after he divorced his fourth wife in 1953. As it happens to most great actors, he could not cope without work: "Without movie parts I was reduced to freak status. I just couldn't stand it." After a withdrawal from drugs and alcohol he recuperated and in 1955 he married a fan, bringing the number of wives to five. He also befriended filmmaker Ed Wood, reputed as the worst director in movie history, and got a part in two of his films. By this time he was not only bankrupt but also felt bitter to miss the big chance of being a versatile artist that he could have been in Hungary. Hollywood's fame was a commercial success, or as he put it: "In Hungary acting is a profession. In America it is a decision." He died virtually forgotten in 1956 and was buried in his Dracula cape in Culver City, California.

Nevertheless, Lugosi has become such a cult figure that no Dracula adaptation (there are more than 160) can ever match his 1931 film. Tim Burton directed a film on Ed Wood's life in 1994 in which Johnny Depp played Ed and Lugosi was cast to Martin Landau. The irony of history is that Landau was so brilliant that it won him the Oscar Lugosi deserved but never managed to get.

Karádi Katalin, Legendary Sex Symbol

Left: Karádi Katalin in 1940
Right: Another photograph of Karádi Katalin in 1940

Commemorative plaque of Katalin Karády in Budapest District V,
Nyáry Pál u. 9

Most nations have a history, Hungarians have Fate. If you want first-hand experience of what this means, go to YouTube and listen to Katalin Karády's melancholy chanson 'Smouldering cigarette end' (Hamvadó cigarettavég). A low decadent voice full of eroticism, a woman in her late twenties with a seductive appearance, who made men crazy and even made well-brought up ladies become maniacal followers of fashion. The male victims of this femme fatale included a tax officer thirty years her senior, who became her first and only husband. Her real love, however, was the Gestapo's top wanted person and head of Hungarian military intelligence during World War II.

Born in 1910 as the seventh child of a messy working-class family, her first and utmost ambition was to get out of poverty and the terror of her father, a compulsive horse racing gambler. Her name, Kanczler was too German-sounding for a media career in Hungary and it was Karády's lucky star, Zoltán Egyed, an influential journalist, who "invented" her as an actress and who later became her impresario. In 1938 he suggested she Hungarianize her name to Karády; after which he created her image as an actress. After a mediocre debut on stage she burst onto the film scene a year later becoming a celebrity almost overnight with the film "Deadly Spring" (Halálos tavasz), not a film of particular artistic value, one of a dozen the Budapest film studios produced in assembly line fashion. The film went almost unnoticed, but thanks to the very influential Catholic Church it became a box-office hit. What inspired the clerics to brand it immoral and detrimental to Christian young people and family values was the not so subtle eroticism Karády produced.

The defenders of pure morals were right in this case. Like Marilyn Monroe, Karády broke sexual taboos. Contrary to the typical female film figures of the day she appeared not as a dumb, sentimental character but a flesh and blood seducer, smoking a cigarette and even wearing trousers. She immediately created fashion, her hairstyle was imitated by hundreds of thousands, her hats became extremely trendy and Karády Fan Clubs were set up all over the country, their members recognized by the Karády collar on their dress.

In the following six years she starred in 22 Hungarian Hollywood-style films and her popularity lasted until the end of the war. She was the leading singing star of the era. Her songs abounded in terms related to fate ("that caused the fall for both of us;" "you can't escape your fate" etc.). The song "Somewhere in Russia" was a sad lyrical memento to the Hungarian soldiers who perished on Russian soil. The style and effect of the song is reminiscent of the similar one during the war by Marlene Dietrich .

What was the secret of her six-year fame? She began her career in 1939 just when Poland was crushed and Hungary opened its borders to hundreds of thousands of Polish refugees. The Hungarian elite was too complacent and short-sighted to foresee that only six years later the price for siding with Hitler would be a country devastated and again truncated, with enormous loss of life. Hungarians were starving for someone to express the Zeitgeist of the era: doom, yielding to Fate, apathy and fear of what may come.

Her career came to an end abruptly after the German occupation of the country in 1944 when the Gestapo held her for months, interrogating her about her connections with pro-Ally contacts, especially István Újszászy, Admiral

Horthy's close associate and head of military intelligence. Unlike her brief marriage and countless love affairs her relationship with Újszászy, a most intelligent and handsome man, was not only passionate but fatal as well. He was arrested the same day as Karády, and later released only to be captured by the Russian army eight months later. She never recovered from the loss of her fiancé. She used her contact with Újszászy to save Jews by organizing their release and hiding them in her villas, of which she had many. In 2004 the Israeli Government awarded her the title of Righteous Person.

After the war she was neglected as an actress. The new communist elite saw her as the representative of a bygone era. Not finding her role under the new regime she decided to flee the country in 1951, leaving everything behind including relatives who were persecuted because of her defection. She settled in Brazil, as at the height of Cold War hysteria in the US she was not granted an American visa. Only 17 years later was she allowed to settle in New York where she ran a fashionable hat shop and lived as a recluse until her death in 1990. She was adamant that she should maintain her legend and never allowed herself to be photographed. Even when her nostalgic revival was at its height in Hungary in the 1980s she still refused to return to Hungary.

But the nation held on to its myths, she was the one thing worth remembering from the war. Eleven days after her death in New York her coffin arrived in Budapest and was displayed in St.Stephen's Basilica. Tens of thousands attended her solemn funeral which reminded people of her famous lines:

Don't ask who I was

I've asked for my fate,

So when it's all enough

I'll be saying adieu.

———————————————

Ferenc Puskás, Everybody's Little Brother

Left: Puskás at Real Madrid (1960s)
Right: Ferenc Puskás during a football match between Amsterdam and Budapest in 1954

The "Golden Team" in 1953 (Ferenc Puskás in the front row, middle)

Before some dimwit in the Ministry of Tourism invented the image of "goulash and the Great Plains" to advertise Hungary abroad, the person who helped foreigners put Hungary on the map was Ferenc Puskás. Even in faraway places like Mombasa, when I explained "Hungary and not hungry" to waiters, they said "ah, Puskas".

His name became known to the world after Hungary's historic football victory of 6-3 in Wembley in 1953. The Magical Magyars - as the British sports press referred to them - were the first Continental team to defeat England on home ground. The mastermind behind the victory was Ferenc Puskás, or as he is known to all Hungarians 'Puskás Öcsi'. This nickname, Öcsi (pronounced 'urtchee'), reveals everything about his character, and explains how he become an icon for the nation. In Hungarian, "öcsi" is the name given to a younger brother and is reserved for family use. However, when a whole country calls someone by this nickname it implies that he is one of us, the beloved younger brother.

Born into a poor working class family in 1927, his football career began in empty urban plots between blocks which we call 'grund'. Football has always been the sport of the poor, as no special equipment was needed (not even a proper leather ball, as any ball-like thing passed). If you were talented you could make a swift career. And Öcsi was talented, so much so that he played for the adult club of Kispest at the age of 16 (he falsified his real age). His real debut was in August 1945, just four months after the country was liberated from German occupation, when he received his first cap against Austria (5-2). He played 84 more times in Hungarian colours and scored 84 goals - just one of the innumerable records he set in football history.

The highlight of his career was of course the match at Wembley in which he scored two goals, the second the legendary drag back as he tricked Billy Wright and scored the fourth Hungarian goal with his left foot. The Hungarian "underdogs" made the Hungarian public euphoric and English football management self-critical. In Hungary victory was not just seen as a sports success, but a remedy for all the suffering meted out during the terrible dictatorship of Mátyás Rákosi, Stalin's best pupil. Puskás and the Golden Team became the national heroes, at least until the 1954 World Cup Final in Bern, when the stars of the event were defeated 3-2 by an underrated German (then West-German) team. Just like the earlier victory, the defeat was blown up out of all proportion by the Hungarian public. Even today people refer to it as a national tragedy comparable only to the disasters of Mohács and Trianon.

And then came the 1956 revolution. The Golden Team left for Spain and only a few players returned. Puskás himself chose "the free world" and thus became a pariah of the political regime that followed under Kádár János. After recuperating from the shock of exile from his homeland, he rebuilt his football career at Real Madrid and became known as "Pancho" to the Spanish. After finishing his career as a player he wandered from country to country as a trainer in Chile, Paraguay, Egypt, Canada, and Australia, but his most notable success was in Greece where he assisted Panathinaikos to a series of victories.

He returned to Hungary for good in 1991 only to live off the fruits of a long career and live out his days as the legend the

Hungarians needed so much. Though his adulation might have gone a little too far (naming the national stadium after him during his lifetime) he coped with popularity in a jovial and no-nonsense manner. This answers the enigma of how a man whose only talent was to kick balls became a national icon. The secret is – and many modern overnight celebs should learn from him – that he remained the same anti-authoritarian, loveable, generous person that he was when playing on the grunds of Kispest. He died after a long struggle against Alzheimer's disease in 2006, and received a grandiose funeral.

Vagabonds

Móric Benyovszky, The Hungarian Made King of Madagascar

Left: 18th century engraving of Móric Benyovszky
Right: Front page of "Memoirs and Travels of Mauritius Augustus count de Benyovszky", 1790

Cover Page of the "Protocolle Du Regiment Des Volontaire De Benyowszky"

We Hungarians like travelling, and no tsunami, earthquake or suicide bomber can deter us. In December I was the tour leader for a Hungarian group to India, and our itinerary included Mumbai. Then came the terrorist attack on the Taj Mahal Hotel. No one in the group voted to change our planned route, even though more than 50% of American and Western tourists had made cancellations.

Perhaps the reason why we are so desperate to travel is that we are a landlocked country, but there are also historical motivations. Great Hungarian travelers, explorers and adventurers are assigned a special place in the national pantheon of Hungarian heroes. The word "adventurer" echoes matters of national pride to Hungarian ears. At school, all Hungarian children start learning about Hungarian history from the first chapter called "The Adventures of the Hungarians' between 895 and 955, from the time of the Hungarian conquest of the Carpathian basin until the defeat of the Hungarian nomadic hordes at Augsburg. Hungarian adventures included surprise attacks, looting, and the raping of nuns. As a consequence of our 'adventures' in Europe, the appeal of the day was "Lord, save us from the arrows of the Hungarians". When I first saw in an English source that our adventures were labeled as 'raids', I was shocked and indignant. Nevertheless, this romantic self-image is persistent among my fellow countrymen.

Count Benyovszky is my favourite hero because he embodies all the qualities Hungarians consider a virtue; such as shrewd intelligence, laconism (disregarding the consequences), chivalry, entrepreneurship and inventiveness. These qualities became apparent during his short but hyperactive lifetime. Due to family reasons, Benyovszky deserted the Austrian army and became a freedom fighter for the Polish against the Russians, of which his family was linked, and was later imprisoned in Kamchatka. There he became the confidante of the camp commander, made explorations for thermal springs, and then organized a rebellion, after which he managed to escape and sail as far as the shores of Alaska (Aleut islands), Japan, Formosa (Taiwan) and finally Macao. Through the French consul in Macao he made contact with Louis XV, who gave him permission to establish a French colony in Madagascar. He did more than a good job: he found common ground with the natives and made peace between rival tribes who elected him as their king.

Due to jealous French officialdom he eventually had to leave his natives and return to Europe. His reckless nature inspired him to partake in further adventures. He strove tenaciously to find funding for another expedition to Madagascar, which he got - after being rejected by the French, the British and the Habsburg courts - with the help of some Baltimore businessmen. This time, at the age of 40, he found himself fighting the French with the support of the natives to establish an independent Madagascar, and he died in battle from a French bullet.

His legacy includes a bestseller of the time that was translated into several languages (Memoirs and Travels of Mauritius Augustus count de Benyovszky, London, 1790) and he became the source of inspiration for numerous romanticised novels; even an opera and more recently a film, *Vivát Benyovszky!*, of which the script is based on his escape from Kamchatka.

The things that make him a favourite for Hungarians, Slovaks and Poles are his love for freedom, his unrepentant fame as a rebel, his thirst for exploration and his reputation as a charmer. As for me, there are very few destinations left where I crave to go, but Madagascar is on the top of the list. Not the wildlife and beaches but to walk along Rue Benyowski in Antananarivo, sit in a local bar, watch passersby, and perhaps ask them what they know about the street's peculiar name.

Rózsa Sándor, The King of the Betyárs

Left: Sándor Rózsa's portrait
Right Csongrád County boss Communication: 10,000 forints head-money for Sándor Rózsa (1856)

Left: Rózsa Sándor in the Kufstein Prison (1859-1865)
Right: Cell of Rózsa Sándor at Kufstein Fortress

"Rózsa Sándor" is a household name for Hungarians that recalls commendable national attributes. In many traditional Hungarian restaurants, foreigners will encounter his name when seeing his favourite dish on the menu (roast pork with a slice of bacon served on "tócsni", a roasted potato dumpling). The paradox is that Rózsa Sándor was a criminal: a highwayman, rebel, outcast, or "betyár" as Hungarians called them in the mid-19th century. This word is difficult to translate, as its English equivalents often carry negative associations, while the word "betyár" has a positive connotation that is deeply ingrained in the national psyche. "Betyár honesty" for example, refers to standing by someone even if s/he has committed a serious infringement of the rules or laws. Rózsa Sándor's romanticized figure symbolizes the Hungarian anti-establishment, a rebellious attitude, and a strong sense of dignity. Together these sentiments play an important role in the ways we handle everyday affairs.

Biographical details reveal that Rózsa was a daring, impoverished man who turned to a life of brigandage. Born in 1813 on the Great Plain, his childhood was harsh. His father was hanged for stealing a horse, and this provided him with the behavioural patterning (as today's psychologists might put it) that led him into the murky world of cow theft at the age of 23. He was jailed in the infamous Szeged "Star" prison, but managed to escape, becoming a runaway betyár who spent his life in constant hiding. The legend of Rózsa "taking from the rich and giving to the poor" was established around this time. His charismatic yet bloody rise to fame led to his being pardoned by the Revolutionary Kossuth Government in

1848 on the condition that he joined the rebellion with a small (but fearsome) contingent of 150 outlaws. However, after a few successful raids on the pro-Habsburg Serbians, it became apparent that leopards do not change their spots: his gang focused more on looting than the fight for freedom. The group was officially disbanded, even though Rózsa's support for Kossuth had made him famous among the people as a freedom fighter.

After the failure of the revolution in 1849 Rózsa went back to his old ways. He was captured in 1857, but even the oppressive Austrian authorities were afraid to execute such a popular figure, and he was given a life sentence instead. He spent 9 years in a string of Austrian prisons, but was freed in 1868 as part of a general political amnesty, an imperial gesture to the Hungarians after the 1867 Compromise. He should have appreciated his luck, but old habits die hard, and he neglected the opportunity to return to a "normal" lifestyle, even though the years were slowly catching up on him. In 1869 Baron Ráday was appointed by the Court to eliminate rural vandalism and secure law and order. He managed to catch the living legend after a train robbery, and this time Rózsa was imprisoned for good. Nine years later the most famous of the betyárs died of tuberculosis. He had become a morose and solitary man.

Rózsa Sándor became an emblematic national icon because his character encapsulated the Hungarian yearning for freedom from authority (which until recently happened to be foreign: not long after the Habsburg administration, which was run by cronies, came German influence, and then a pervasive network of Russian control). Perhaps the Hungarian penchant for outsmarting the authorities can be traced back this set of circumstances. Even today, manifestations of this attitude are abundant. Just think of the grey economy. A more subtle example might be the unique system of ticket control on Budapest's public transport network. "Fare dodging" is still a national sport, and you're actually given a chance in the catch-me-if-you-can game between passengers and BKV inspectors, the indirect descendants of the gendarmes in Rózsa Sándor's time. There was even a modern day Rózsa Sándor in 1999, the so-called "Whisky Robber" who was hailed as a folk hero as he frequently outwitted the police. The result of all this is that the fall guys are often policemen or other authority figures: the time-worn joke of "how many [insert victim of choice] do you need to change a light bulb?" can be translated into Hungarian as "how many policemen do you need to...?"

Whether you like outlaws or not, do not miss Rózsa's favourite dish when you next go to a Hungarian restaurant.

Ágoston Haraszty, The Father of California Wine

Left: Portrait of the Hungarian Count Ágoston Haraszthy
Right: Wooden carving from 1889 on the front part of a barrel at
Buena Vista Winery (still used as the winery's logo)

From Haraszty's book: "Grape culture, wines, and wine-making"
(1862)

The best lesson I had with my American students back at Rutgers University was the wine tasting class where I was supposed to teach them about Hungarian culture. Blindfolded, they had to guess which wine was Californian and which was Hungarian; they kept guessing until the last drop and in the end everyone turned out to be a winner. As I explained to the students, the wine could be either Hungarian or Californian, since thanks to a man named Agoston Haraszty, Californian wine was Hungarian as well. It was with this little trick that I managed to put Hungary on their mental map.

Agoston Haraszty became a legend in the United States, especially in California. In 1969, at the centennial of Haraszty's death Ronald Reagan, then Governor of California, praised him by saying, "Colonel Ágoston Haraszthy can well be called the father of the wine industry in California. ..."

The problem with legendary figures, however, is that there is always a counter-legend. It can't be truer in this case; Haraszthy was neither a colonel, nor the father of California wine. True, he joined the Royal Hungarian Guard of Francis I in 1830 at the age of 18 but after two years of service he went back to the family estate in Futak, in the south of Hungary (now Serbia). Only a year later he married Eleonora Dedinszky, a noble of Polish descent who bore him six children in less than a decade. Though he served in the Hungarian Diet representing his region, his dedication to the national reformist movement lead by Széchenyi and later Kossuth, was superseded by his keen interest in America.

In 1840 Haraszty set out on a well-planned trip to explore America, which would result in a travelogue entitled *Utazások Éjszakamerikában* (Travels in North America), published in Pest in 1844. Still an enjoyable read, it was only the second of its kind about America to reach the Hungarian public, following Bölöni-Farkas's work under a similar title published in 1833.

Mesmerized by the beauty of the landscape he bought land west of Madison, Wisconsin where he moved his family and parents after selling his properties in Hungary in 1842. True to his pioneering spirit he embarked on a multitude of activities: He planned and built a city which he named Széptáj (meaning: beautiful landscape, now called Sauk City), built a sawmill, raised hops, set up a brickyard, operated a ferry and steamboat on the Wisconsin River and for the first time he experimented with the grapevines he brought from Hungary. The latter turned out to be a failure due to winter frosts.

Elected captain of a wagon train, his adventurous spirit drove him to pack up his family in 1849 and head for California via the Santa Fe Trail. Haraszty chose to settle in San Diego which had a population of a mere 650 people and in no time plunged into town planning and numerous business enterprises and planted a vineyard. Little wonder he was soon elected sheriff of San Diego County and in 1851 he was sent to the California State Assembly.

Haraszty's career in the legislature did not stop him from engaging in various business activities including starting the Eureka Gold and Silver Refinery and relentless experimentation with cultivating wine grapes. After repeated failures he finally found fertile ground in Sonoma, north of San Francisco, where he bought a vineyard and named it Buena Vista, the Spanish version of Széptáj back in Wisconsin. By 1861, less than five years after the purchase, he turned his estate into the most prosperous vineyard in California by importing thousands of vines of more than one hundred varieties.

His flamboyant lifestyle and inexhaustible energy to meet challenges brought him as many friends as enemies. The latter, especially those interested in wine production, kept accusing him of building up his own legend. Nevertheless, the success story came to a sudden end in 1866 when Haraszty was forced to resign from the management of the Viticultural Society he founded due to lack of profits caused by an outbreak of phylloxera infestation.

Like a phoenix rising Haraszty started again in 1868 at the age of 56. After selling his remaining property he went to Nicaragua and set up a sugar plantation to make rum and sell it to the American markets; this last plan, however, remained unfinished. His wife died of yellow fever soon after their arrival and in the following year he met his death by being dragged down by an alligator when he tried to cross a river near his plantation.

In the long line of Hungarian travelers, adventurers and explorers Ágoston Haraszty takes a distinguished place as an archetypal figure of entrepreneurial spirit against all odds.

Ignaz Trebitsch, The Talented Mr. Trebitsch

Portrait from circa 1910-1915

Trebitsch-Lincoln as Chao Kung (1943)

While preparing for a trip to Burma (Myanmar these days) I came across an interesting piece of Buddhist literature entitled "The Enigma of Life" whose author was a certain Venerable Chao Kung (meaning "the Light of the Universe"). The author must have been held in great esteem by the Buddhists since he was given a grand funeral in Japanese-occupied Shanghai in 1943. According to an eyewitness, the funeral march was attended by more than one hundred thousand people including Buddhist dignitaries and Japanese high officials.

The real enigma, however, is whether it really was I.T.T. Lincoln −that was his real name −who was buried on that October day, since he was reported to have been seen in Darjeeling four years later. To complicate things further, Ignatius Timothy Tribich-Lincoln was the name he liked to call himself before he was ordained as a Buddhist monk in 1925, but in possession of at least twenty passports, he had as many aliases, befitting a professional international spy and adventurer, which he in fact was. The details of his life abound in mysteries and half-truths, including his c.v. entitled 'The Autobiography of an Adventurer,' which is more of a camouflage to hide the real story. But who was the 'Real Trebitsch', the person behind many guises?

What we know for sure is that he was born Ignaz Trebitsch in 1870 in Paks, South of Hungary, a child of a well-to-do Jewish grain trader. When he was 17 the family moved to Pest, a city buzzing with excitement. No wonder the young Ignaz soon gave up his ambition to become a rabbi for an actress called Ella. His infuriated father - in want of a better idea - sent him to London and that's where his transformations started.

The long line of his metamorphoses started with his baptism by the Irish Presbyterians in 1899, where he took up ministry and was sent to Montreal on a mission to convert Jews fleeing the pogroms in Russia and Eastern Europe. Shortly after, Trebitsch left the Presbyterians for the Anglicans (they promised him a higher salary) and returned to England to occupy his post as a minister in Appledore, Kent granted by no other than the Archbishop of Canterbury. Having got bored of an uneventful life in the English countryside, he abandoned his parish work (to the great relief of the archbishop) and decided that it was politics where he could utilise his talents best.

His political career was made smooth by a chocolate millionaire who was a close associate of Lloyd George and Churchill. Trebitsch became his private secretary, changed his name to the more English sounding I.T.T. Lincoln and against all political odds he won the seat of a most conservative constituency for the Liberal Party in 1908. His role as an MP was short-lived but most profitable. After some failed efforts in the oil business he offered his services to the British Intelligence as a spy but was turned down since the British found out he was playing a double game by flirting with the German intelligence.

He got deeply offended by the British rejection and left for the USA in 1915 where he published a bestseller: *Confessions of an International Spy*, in which he blamed the British for the breakout of the war. After some media stardom in New York Trebitsch was extradited to the British who jailed him for fraud for three years.

In 1919 we find our political Houdini in Berlin as one of the chief architects of the aborted extreme rightist Kapp Putsch hailed by Hitler, who refused to meet him when he realised he was a Jew. His close contacts with the German militarists led to his involvement in a conspiracy to create a Bavarian-Austrian-Hungarian-Prussian confederacy under right-wing rule. In this role he met Admiral Horthy in person in 1920, but after he found out that his fellow-conspirators tried to assassinate him (or so he claims), Trebitsch sold all the compromising files to the Czechoslovakian government and an international scandal broke out.

His final metamorphosis occurred only three years later in Shanghai. He converted to Buddhism and became a respected authority while continuing his multifaceted espionage for the Japanese, Germans, Chinese and most probably the Americans. In typical fashion, Trebitsch could not resist the opportunity to claim he was the reincarnation of the Dalai Lama when the latter died in 1938.

The key to the Trebitsch enigma lies in his exceptional talent to tell people what they wanted to hear, let it be religion, politics or media, to profit from the opportunity and escape at the right moment. That's what our Trebitsch, a mercenary of faith, developed to the level of an art; he was unscrupulous, amoral, corrupt and cynical, but after all he just held a mirror to all those he cheated.

The cause of his death is as much a mystery as most details of his life. Most probably the German espionage poisoned him. Years before his death he sent a dedicated book of his to Regent Miklós Horthy, with a request to return to Hungary, but received no answer. This last gesture of his ensures his place among famous Hungarians, albeit, far from being a great one.

László Almássy, The Hungarian Patient

Left: Portrait of young László Almássy (1915)
Right: Bust of László Almásy in the Hungarian Geographical
Museum, Érd, Hungary

At Wadi Sora - in the center Eppler, Almasy and Stansteade

"Operation Salaam" at Wadi Sura

Count Almásy was a most controversial Hungarian who gained world fame through the 9 Oscar-winning film, the "English Patient" in 1995. The film, based on Michael Ondaatje's novel of the same title, launched an avalanche of articles and studies on László Almásy exploring the differences between the fictitious and the real Count. Although it was pretty clear that the Almásy of the English Patient is the product of Ondaatje's imagination, passions rose high, and the writer was criticized for falsifying history. Western historians – in an endeavour to show the real-life László Almásy – labelled him a Nazi spy and a treacherous figure. Hungarians, however, tend to see him as one of the great explorers and an esteemed cartographer, while the Egyptians respect him as the "Father of deserts", the name given to him by a camel driver. *Jebel Almasy*, the Saharan Mountain, and *Al-Mazi* the sports aviation airport of Cairo, are both named after him.

Let's leave Ondaatje's English patient and see what might have caused all this controversy. I'd rather call the real László Almásy the *Hungarian* Patient (sorry, Mr. Ondaatje), since he embodies several character traits that Hungarians, especially of his generation, are famous for: thirst for adventure, stubborn patriotism, recklessness and chivalry. If it hadn't been for Rommel and his Afrika Korps, Almásy would have been noted as a motorist, a pioneering explorer of the Sahara, and an excellent cartographer.

Born into an aristocratic but untitled family in 1895 (they never received the title of Count due the collapse of the Austro-Hungarian Monarchy in 1918 – thus "count" is in inverted commas), his affinity with birds and metal birds, i.e. planes, showed early. He made his debut on the Russian front as an officer for the Hungarian Royal Air Force in World War I. After failing in a melodramatic attempt to reclaim the Hungarian throne for Franz Joseph's grandnephew, King Karl IV, (he drove the king's car to Budapest) he decided there was no future for him in his truncated country, and accepted an offer to test drive cars in the Sahara for Steyr, an Austrian car manufacturer. Steyr must have been pleased with his skills, as the company financed several expeditions, and Almásy explored lands in Egypt, Libya and the Sudan. His knowledge of the Sahara enabled him to join Sir Robert Clayton's expedition to find the legendary lost Oasis of Zarzura in 1932. Several other expeditions followed, which led to the discovery of some notable prehistoric rock art sites and a substantial collection of maps.

However, it was his skill as a cartographer that eventually led to his demise. After World War II broke out in 1939 he had to leave Egypt and return to Hungary. Two years later, the Germans discovered his knowledge of the area (and his collection of maps), and as a reserve officer of the Hungarian Air Force he "was lent" to the Wehrmacht to serve in Rommel's Afrika Korps. Under the command of Rommel and Admiral Canaris he conducted a daring mission called "Operation Salaam", and spirited two German agents across more than 3,000 kilometres from Tripoli to Egypt, deep behind Allied lines. In recognition of his services, Rommel not only promoted him, but also awarded him the Iron Cross. Yet Almásy's success was to backfire: in 1946 he was accused by the People's Tribunal in Budapest of being a Nazi collaborator. Released without charge, he was reputedly smuggled out of Hungary with the assistance of British intelligence, and went back to Cairo. He died six years later in Salzburg where he was buried with the exact details of his wartime role left unclear.

László Almásy's story is a typical Hungarian story. In a country where not less than seven changes of regime occurred in about 70 years (revolutions, counter-revolutions, occupations and dictatorship), his life reflects the difficulties faced by many in a world of shifting loyalties. All this turmoil in the span of one lifetime left us with countless Hungarian patients; Almásy's story is merely one notable example amongst many.

Unbridled Geniuses

Arthur Koestler, A Man of Causes

Left: Photograph of Arthur Koestler in 1969
Right: 1st US edition of *Darkness at Noon* (Cover)

Arthur Koestler's life-size bronze statue sculpted by Imre Varga in
Budapest (Városligeti fasor 2)

Even today I feel a cramp in my stomach at the sight of a customs officer asking, "Any goods to declare?" since the bygone Communist regime made us all smugglers. Books banned in Hungary could be purchased free of charge at a small bookshop near St. Paul's Cathedral in London upon showing a passport from any Communist country. Among the hottest items was Arthur Koestler's *Darkness at Noon.* Given the subject matter of the book that brought him world fame and his subsequent campaigns against Stalinist regimes, it's no surprise he became enemy number one in the Soviet Union and was banned in his native Hungary until the collapse of the regime in 1989.

Darkness at Noon was born out of 20 years of his diverse personal experiences. During these two decades he joined two utopian causes, Zionism and Communism (only to experience their futility). Faced his impending execution on death row in Spain, Koestler spent months in a French concentration camp and a few more in a British prison as a resident alien.

Born in Budapest into a middle-class Jewish family in 1905 Koestler was socialized into Hungarian culture. When he was 14 the family moved to Vienna and since felt he spent the rest of his life, as he put it, "in exile from Central Europe." A search for identity may have lain behind his passion to continually embrace new causes. He terminated his studies in Vienna in 1926 to go to Palestine enraptured by the charisma of Vladimir Jabotinsky, leader of the militant wing of Zionism. However, deeply disappointed in the utopian kibbutz movement and fanatical followers of Judaism, he left for Paris three years later and then moved to Berlin to work as a journalist for German newspapers. It was there in 1931 that he joined the Communist Party of Germany, assuming it was the best means to fight the rising tide of fascism.

The following year he managed to get permission to travel throughout the Soviet Union. Though his high expectations concerning the achievements of the five-year plan were crushed by the reality of everyday life, he remained a member of the Party. In 1936 Koestler was sent to Spain by the Comintern on a clandestine mission to find evidence for German and Italian support for the Franco forces. A year later he was caught by the Nationalists and sentenced to death; only through intense international protest and an exchange of prisoners he avoided execution. Koestler documented the trauma of his captivity in the book *Dialogue with Death*.

The large-scale show trials in Moscow and the Ribbentrop-Molotov Pact led him to abandon all illusions he had about Communism and leave the Party in 1938. The result of his disenchantment with Communism was *Darkness at Noon*, which was first published in London in 1940.

The outbreak of the Second World War found him in Vichy France where he was interned because he still held a Hungarian passport. He managed to escape from the concentration camp only by joining the French Foreign Legion, then defected in Marseille, and through Lisbon he reached England to seek asylum. England became his adopted country for the rest of his life where he received British citizenship in 1945.

He continued to be a prolific writer, published 30 books, novels, essays and an autobiography. In 1950 he was instrumental in founding the CIA sponsored *Congress for Cultural Freedom* to counterbalance Soviet peace propaganda but five years later gave up on all political activities. In a frenzied new quest for identity Koestler pursued a wide range of activities. After a trip to Japan and India he concluded that eastern spiritualism cannot provide complete answers to western societies' needs (*The Lotus and the Robot*, 1960); after meeting Timothy Leary in New York he concluded that hallucinogens were also not the answer (*Return Trip to Nirvana*, 1967); he also launched campaigns for the abolition of capital punishment and for legalizing euthanasia. In addition, he devoted most of his creative energies to scientific research, especially on telepathy. His devotion to mysticism lead him to leave his entire property to found a Chair of Parapsychology at the Edinburgh University before he arranged his own suicide in 1983 when his leukemia reached a critical stage. His wife Cynthia, though in good health, joined him in desperation.

Koestler's legacy was not only the documenting of the political and intellectual challenges of the 20th century but also making a difference through his own activism. In honour of his memory a statue was erected at the Edinburgh University. It was removed in 1993 after a disputable biography on him was published accusing him of alleged rapes and philandering. Nevertheless, his home city awarded him a memorial statue at Lövölde tér in 2009, next to the house where he was born. More than a century later he is back where he belongs.

László Bíró, The Man Who Gave His Name to a Pen

Left: László Bíró on the wall of building u4 in the Graphisoft Park, Budapest (Gázgyár Street)
Right: Advertising in Argentine magazine Leoplán promoting the first commercial ballpoint pen, brand "birome" (1945)

Commemorative plaque of László Bíró (Budapest D. II, Cimbalom utca 12)

Whenever I travel to less developed parts of the world, such as Cambodia, I always take hundreds of ballpoint pens with me for convenience. The reason is that hordes of children will nag you for a pen: "pen, Sir, gimme a pen". If it were not for language difficulties I would tell them that this useful item was invented by a Hungarian called László Bíró; his surname is still the generic name used for the ballpoint pen in most English-speaking countries.

The story behind what today is an everyday item is most fascinating. Bíró, born in Budapest in 1899, embodies many of the features Hungarians are renowned for: ingenuity, craftiness, Bohemianism, naivety, and good survival skills. The first skill on the list became manifest after he was conscripted during World War I: he quickly escaped with his buddies and went into hiding in Budapest. His wide range of interests drove him to study hypnosis at the University of Medicine, but after an ill-fated experiment he gave up and worked as a customs officer for an oil company. He then took up painting, and for a change he bought a Bugatti and even won a car race. In 1932 he finally landed the post of the editor for the journal "Hongrie-Magyarország-Hungary". His irritation at the constant smudging and dripping of fountain pens led him to the invention of the ball-point pen. As a gifted painter he was fascinated by the rolling of blobs of ink to make a continuous line. The rest was a question of technical implementation to find the ideal size of ball and cartridge, and the right kind of ink. He patented his invention in 1938, but it took him seven more years of experimentation to perfect the design.

Under normal circumstances this would have been the beginning of a great success story. However, the words 'Hungary' and 'normal' are contradictory terms. On January 1 1939, as part of anti-Jewish legislation, a law was passed prohibiting the movement of intellectual property out of the country. Bíró left for Paris the day before. After the German occupation of France he continued his flight to Argentina, where he remained for the rest of his life. His new choice of homeland was influenced by an accidental encounter with Agustín P. Justo at a spa in the Adriatic back in 1938. The Argentinian was fascinated by Bíró's invention, and invited him to Argentina to pursue his experiments. His business card simply stated 'President', and it was only at the Argentinian Consulate in Paris that Bíró realized he was not the president of some obscure company, but president of the country. His adopted country treated him well, and every year Inventors' Day is celebrated on his birthday.

As an inventor he was very productive. He is credited with hundreds of technical inventions and innovations, including roll-on deodorant (no sweat after the ball-point pen), the steam-powered washing machine, and automatic transmission devices for cars. The latter was bought by General Motors, but only to prevent their competitors getting hold of the invention. GM never paid him his due. And neither did he become a mega millionaire out of the pen that was named after him. Being a lousy businessman, he allowed a certain Mrs Láng, a Hungarian-Argentinian, to rip him off and take his patent rights. Despite all his failures and frustrations with people he never gave up and never gave in to despair.

Bíró is an exceptional figure among the long list of Hungarian inventors for a number of reasons. He never received a PhD or even a university degree, as painting and inventing took up all his creative energy. He kept on working on new inventions until the day he died in 1985 in Buenos Aires. László Bíró is one of the many 'science celebrities' who we Hungarians love to be proud of, but only after they have become famous abroad, and after they have died.

Albert Szent-györgyi, The Man Behind Vitamin C

Left: Photograph of Albert Szent-györgyi (1950)
Right: Albert Szent-györgyi receives the Nobel Prize (Stockholm 1937)

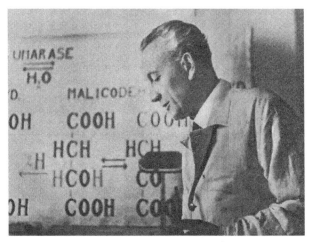

Albert Szent-györgyi with the formula of Vitamin C in the background (1937)

I like eating lecsó (letscho), and love making it. It's in season from June to September, making it the Hungarian summer staple food. The quintessence of this vegetable stew is sweet peppers in all shapes and colours mixed with onions, tomatoes, and paprika-spiced sausage.

Hungarians are crazy about this food not only because it's delicious, but it's incredibly healthy as well. Paprika contains several times more vitamin C than lemons or oranges and we can thank Hungarian scientist Albert Szent-Györgyi for this discovery in 1932, of which he was awarded the Nobel Prize. TIME magazine called it the 'Paprika Prize,' deservedly, since after more than a decade of experimentation Szent-Györgyi discovered the rich vitamin content of the paprika by analyzing it chemically instead of eating it. Although vitamin C is a routine part of our diet today, at the time Szent-Györgyi's findings were revolutionary and innovative as it hindered the development of a disease such as, scurvy, hence vitamin C's official name: 'ascorbic acid.' Famous for his bon-mots and special talent to make science understandable, Szent-Györgyi put it this way, "A vitamin is a substance that makes you ill if you don't eat it."

Known both in academic circles and popular culture mostly for his work with vitamin C, he actually left a larger-than-life size oeuvre behind him when he died at the age of 93. Szent-Györgyi could be considered the last of the great scientists who dedicated himself wholly to scientific truth without commercial compromise. He despised what he called 'technologists' and government funding that demanded an expected result from research. He said 'if I know what the result will be, it's not worth starting it in the first place.'

He lived a full life, and was a well-rounded figure whose unconventional character and amiable personality made him friends all over the world. Three adjectives best characterize his life: reckless, obstinate and curious. A reckless youth, an obstinate free-lancer who never gave in to the lures of either the Russian or the American academic establishment, and most of all, an inquisitive scientist, in his own words: "As a researcher all I did was to satisfy my curiosity."

Born into a well-to-do family in Budapest in 1893, as a child Szent-Györgyi showed no sign of the future genius. On the contrary, he played truant, disliked books and was even considered an idiot, at least by his family's standards according to a memorable interview he gave to BBC in 1965.

A thirst for knowledge gripped him suddenly at the age of 16 when he declared to his maternal uncle, the most famous physiologist at the time in Hungary, that he wished to become a research doctor. In spite of his uncle's resolute discouragement he pursued medical studies and excelled in all possible fields. After studies in Berlin, research in Holland, and numerous publications, at the age of 33 he was renowned enough to be invited to Cambridge by Sir Frederick Gowland Hopkins, a great name in biochemistry.

The highlight of his career is associated with Szeged, the paprika capital of Hungary, where he was awarded a chair at the University, later becoming its President. The Nobel Prize in 1937 made Szent-Györgyi a celebrity and ensured a kind of political immunity, which he very much needed after joining the antifascist resistance in 1943. Later that year he was sent by Count Bethlen, the Hungarian Pro-Allies Prime Minister, to Istanbul under the guise of delivering lectures but in reality to have secret negotiations with the Allies about quitting the country's German allegiance. His covert mission, however, was found out by the Germans and thus he had to go into hiding from the Gestapo for almost two years. Even Regent Horthy was summoned to Klessheim near Salzburg to meet Hitler where the Führer allegedly banged the table and shouted at the Admiral demanding that he extradite the 'Schweinhund Szent-Györgyi.'

After the war he was wooed by the Russians who were considering making him president of the liberated country. However, after two years of active involvement in reorganizing and modernizing the Hungarian Academy of Sciences he broke ties with the ruling communist elite and left the country in 1947. His application to apply for an American visa was not welcomed by the FBI, yet he managed to settle in the United States where he was naturalized in 1955. He bought a large house called Seven Winds in Woods Hole, Massachusetts, where he set up his own laboratory for cancer research. Szent-Györgyi decided not to accept any academic position or government funding to preserve his commitment to independent science and free thinking. Seven Winds became a pilgrimage place for many scientists, and when they visited they were treated with great hospitality typical of Szent-Györgyi. For a few years even anti-war youth horded the place to listen to the anti-military speeches of the professor. As a staunch opponent of the Vietnam War he summed up his views on the moral responsibility of scientists in his book *Crazy Ape* (1970), an important part of his legacy as a humanist and thinker who devoted his life to uncovering the secrets of life.

His native country still holds him in the highest esteem; the Szeged Medical University was named after him following his death in 1986.

Leó Szilárd, Doctor A-bomb

Left: Photograph of Leó Szilárd (circa 1960)
Right: Atomic Cloud Rises Over Nagasaki (1945)

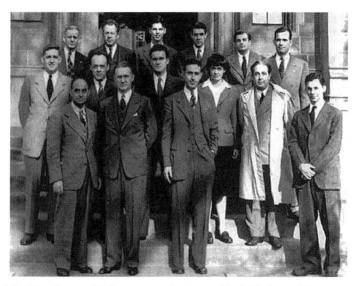

The Metallurgical Laboratory scientists, with Szilárd third from right, in the lab coat (1946)

First time I heard the story of Hungarians being Martians was from Hungarian-Americans in the US who were proud of their roots. The widespread anecdote behind it is that Enrico Fermi, the physicist in charge of the Manhattan Project during World War II, was deliberating on the existence of extraterrestrial intelligent beings and concluded that they surely reached the earth but then where are they? – he posed the question. "They are already here among us: they just call themselves Hungarians" – came the stoic answer from his audience. This witty bon mot, together with hundreds of others is owed to Leó Szilárd, the most colourful and original of the scientists with Hungarian roots who were instrumental in developing the American nuclear program.

The number of Nobel Prize winners per capita has always been a matter of national pride, even though all of these celebrities –with the exception of Albert Szent-Györgyi- were awarded for the achievements they produced in other countries, mostly in the US. However, Leó Szilárd, never received a Nobel Prize for his contribution to nuclear physics, but he is still one of the best representatives of the long line of Hungarian geniuses produced at the beginning of the 20th century.

The Szilárds were a middle-class Jewish family, who Hungarianized their family name from Spitz in 1900, two years after their prodigy son Leó was born. His versatile talent for literature and sciences showed early. After finishing one of the elite Gymnasiums in Budapest he pursued engineering studies at the Technical University. His promising academic career in Hungary was suddenly interrupted by an insult he suffered at the university for his

Jewish ancestry in the wake of the fallen short-lived Communist regime of Béla Kun even though he and his brother had converted to Calvinism before. This outrage of violence made him leave Hungary for good in 1919, marking the beginning of his "flying Dutchman" existence for the rest of his life. Szilárd never had any property apart from two packed suitcases, ready for moving on whenever needed.

His Berlin years were the most productive. His interest turned towards physics and his innovative dissertation on thermodynamics brought him the appreciation of Max von Laue and Albert Einstein. The latter became a lasting friend and they even a shared patent for a new refrigeration system. It was also during these Berlin years when he became life-long friends with the three other Hungarians from Budapest, Eugene Wigner, Edward Teller and John von Neumann forming together in the early 1940s the 'Hungarian Mafia' as Alvin Weinberg, a fellow physicist administering the Manhattan Project, referred to them amiably.

Having learnt the lesson of what rising anti-semitism can lead to, Szilárd acted promptly after Hitler took over and with an acute sense of timing left Berlin on the last train on March 31, 1933 before travel restrictions for Jews were introduced the next day. The same year he settled in London, that is in London hotels, and spent his time thinking. English tolerance for his eccentric manners afforded him the freedom of intellectual rambling. His work methodology was to take long baths, walk and in the meantime think and take notes. Inspired by a lecture of Lord Rutheford, an eminent physicist of the time, he focused all his attention on refuting Rutherford's thesis that atoms cannot be a source of energy. The illumination came while waiting at the traffic lights when red changed to amber and then to green. His turbulent mind translated it to the multiplication of neutrons thus the theory of chain reaction was born which pleased him and at the same time frightened him since he intuitively felt that this conception could lead to the production of a lethal weapon capable of causing unfathomable destruction. To avoid unwarranted use of his discovery he patented his formula with the Admiralty assigning it as a military secret in 1936. This moral dilemma of the role of scientists followed him for the rest of his life. At this time all known scientists considered the nuclear chain reaction to be moonshine, to quote Rutherford, but Niels Bohr and even Fermi with whom he constructed the first nuclear reactor in 1942 thought it was the rambling of a weird mind.

To avoid the imminent war he emigrated to the United States and shared his discovery with Einstein and persuaded him to write a letter to President Roosevelt to warn him how the A-bomb could determine the outcome of the war. As a consequence the President set up the Manhattan Project and the race for priority with the Germans started. After the two A-bombs were completed in Los Alamos, Szilard launched a campaign to stop the dropping of bombs on Japanese cities. After the unexpected death of Roosevelt his efforts turned futile with his successor Truman.

After the tragedy of Hiroshima he abandoned nuclear physics and turned to microbiology as a scientist, but most of his time was devoted to political activism to stop the arms race between the US and the Soviet Union. He was the soul of the Pugwash conferences of scientists initiated by Einstein and Bertrand Russell aiming at the peaceful use of atomic energy. He even had a meeting with Khrushchev bombarding him with unorthodox ideas to curb armament. Two years before his untimely death in 1964 he founded the Council for a Livable World to put pressure on Congress to harness nuclear weapons. His ceaseless fight for a peaceful world brought attention to the vulnerability of scientists by warning them that their political indifference and lack of moral stature can assist the army and politics can abuse their results.

Leo Szilard's greatness can best be summed up by his own ironic reflection that he and Fermi should have been awarded the Nobel Prize for NOT having conducted uranium experiments in the early 1930s. Otherwise we would be living in a completely different world.

Pál Erdős, The Vagabond of Mathematics

Left: Portrait of Pál Erdős in 1992
Right: Pál Erdős' tomb at the Jewish Cemetery in Budapest, Kozma Street

Paul Erdős teaching 10-year-old mathematical child prodigy Terence Tao in 1985, at the University of Adelaide

Being called to the blackboard to prove a mathematic equation is still a horror for most students in Hungarian schools; they definitely were for me. I managed only thanks to my "bench-mate" who helped me with my math exercises in return for my assistance in doing his Russian homework. Later, mathematicians became the object of my envy. Considering themselves the aristocrats of sciences they seemed to live in another world undisturbed from the trivialities of everyday life. No wonder the archetypal figure of an absent-minded or eccentric professor is most often a mathematician. Pál Erdős is the perfect example.

Erdős was destined to be a mathematician. He was born into a Jewish family as Pál Engländer in 1913. His parents, who were both teachers of mathematics, discovered the child prodigy in him when he was only three. His inability to deal with practical issues as an adult may have been rooted in his overprotective childhood. His two sisters died of scarlet fever just a few days before he was born. His mother, whom he called "Anyuka" (diminutive of "Mama" in Hungarian) his whole life, provided private tutoring just to protect him from the harm of the outside world. By the age of 20 he discovered a simple proof for a classic theorem of number theory, which brought him international fame. His lifetime achievements are indisputable in various fields of mathematics: combinatorics, graph theory, number theory, classical analysis, approximation theory, set theory, and probability theory.

The secret of his productiveness lay not only in his ingenious mind but also in his life philosophy, non-conformist lifestyle and charismatic personality. Having acquired his doctorate at the age of 21 he took a postdoctoral fellowship in Manchester. Four years later the once-in-a-lifetime opportunity arrived when he got a one-year fellowship at Princeton, which could have set him on a secure career path in academia. However, the Princeton elite found him "uncouth and unconventional" and refused to renew his stay at the university in 1939.

This unexpected move made him a vagabond, a professor with two suitcases and no address, no telephone number or credit card. The breakout of World War II made it impossible for him to return to Europe and his zig-zagging between universities and conferences became his habitual lifestyle. He was most attached to Purdue and Notre Dame, the latter even offering him a permanent status which he could never take due to his expulsion from the United States in 1954. Of the most colourful FBI files on Erdős, is the legend circulating that includes of him ignoring a 'No trespassing' sign near a radar station on Long Island when he was walking with two other colleagues deeply involved in conversation about the possible solutions of a theorem. He was allowed back in the US only after 1961.

In the meantime he developed a worldwide network of mathematicians, posing problems to be solved and often collaborating with them in finding the simplest solution. Since he considered property to be a nuisance, whatever money he received for lecturing and awards, he gave away, mostly to young mathematicians. His 50-to-1000 dollar checks awarded to solve mathematics problems became legendary. Actually, it was not a big financial loss for him since most of these checks were never cashed, but framed, signifying the status of the holder's position in mathematics.

"Pali bácsi," or "Uncle Pali," as most of his students, friends and admirers endearingly addressed him, became a household name in mathematics circles through the coinage of the term "Erdős number" denoting the degree of separation from the beloved mathematician. He was one of the most prolific authors in mathematics with more than 1,500 publications, and one third of his published articles were written in collaboration with a colleague. These individuals could claim an Erdős number of 1 (there are 462 of them), and those who published a joint article with an "Erdős #1" holder could claim to be "Erdős #2" (they amount to a total of 4,560 collaborators—including Einstein), and so on. The highest known Erdős number is 15. By motivating colleagues to collaborate he changed the antagonistic nature of this science from a competition into a network of people sharing efforts in solving problems.

His life and oeuvre are exemplary in many ways. Obsession with science, uncompromising fight for intellectual independence, non-attachment to worldly things like personal comfort, property, fame and social status combined with a disposition to be the giver and very rarely the taker, made him a beloved and influential person in the world of mathematics.

He died in Warsaw with a pen in his hand over his notebook at the break of a conference, deep in his thoughts perhaps about the solving of the next grand theorem. Erdős' grave is in the Kozma Street Jewish Cemetery in Budapest.

Image & Photo Credits

Attila the Hun, Our Hun

- Mór Than's painting The Feast of Attila, based on a fragment of Priscus:
  Mór Than / Wikimedia Commons / Public Domain

- The Empire of the Huns and subject tribes at the time of Attila.
  © Slovenski Volk / Wikimedia Commons / CC-BY-SA-3.0

- Allegorical depiction by Eugène Delacroix (1843–1847) - Title: Attila and his Hordes Overrun Italy and the Arts (detail)).
  Eugène Delacroix / Wikimedia Commons / Public Domain

Chief Árpád, The Founding Father

- Honfoglalás by Mihály Munkácsy
  Mihály Munkácsy/ Wikimedia Commons / Public Domain

- Árpád's statue at the Heroes' Square (Budapest)
  © User:Ealdgyth / Wikimedia Commons / CC BY 3.0 / GFDL

- Statue of Árpád at Ráckeve (Town in Hungary)
  User:Csanády / Wikimedia Commons / Public Domain

Sándor Kőrösi-Csoma, Seeking Hungarian roots, founding Tibetology

- Lithography showing Sándor Kőrösi-Csoma by Schöfft Ágoston
  Schöfft Ágoston User:Csanády / Wikimedia Commons / Public Domain

- Tomb and Memorial in a cemetery of Darjeeling, often garlanded with khatas
  User:Grentidez / Wikimedia Commons / CC0 1.0 / Public Domain

- Route taken by Sándor Kőrösi-Csoma
  © User:L. Shyamal / Wikimedia Commons / CC BY-SA 3.0

Ármin Vámbéry, The Dervish in Disguise

- Portrait of Ármin Vámbéry
  K. Koller / Wikimedia Commons / Public Domain

- Bust at Hungarian Geographical Museum in Érd
  © Elekes Andor / Wikimedia Commons / CC BY-SA 4.0

- Map of the travel of Armin Vambery in Central Asia
  © Lepeltier.ludovic / Wikimedia Commons / CC BY-SA 3.0 / GFDL

Mátyás, The King in Disguise

- Portrait Matthias Corvinus
  © Chris Furkert, user: Samat / Wikimedia Commons / CC BY-SA 3.0 / GFDL

- Matthias Corvinus depicted in the *Chronica Hungarorum*

Johannes de Thurocz / Wikimedia Commons / Public Domain

- Matthias Corvinus Monument in front of St. Michael's Church in Cluj-Napoca, Romania
  © Matei Domnita / Wikimedia Commons / CC BY-SA 2.0

István Széchenyi, The Greatest of the Magyars

- Count István Széchenyi
  Miklós Barabás/ Wikimedia Commons / Public Domain

- Széchenyi on the 5000 Hungarian forint banknote
  © Magyar Nemzeti Bank (Hungarian National Bank) / Wikimedia Commons /

- Széchenyi offers one year's income of his estate to establish and endow the Hungarian Academy of Sciences
  Vinzenz Katzler / Wikimedia Commons / Public Domain

Albert Apponyi, The Architect of Trianon

- Photo of Apponyi Albert (1900)
  Athenaeum R.T. / Wikimedia Commons / Public Domain

- Portrait of Apponyi Albert (1910)
  Veres Ferenc / Wikimedia Commons / Public Domain

- Apponyi in Paris for the Treaty of Trianon; 1920
  Agence de presse Mondial Photo-Presse / Wikimedia Commons / Public Domain

Mihály Károlyi, The Red Count

- Photo of Mihály Károlyi (1923)
  Veres / Wikimedia Commons / Public Domain

- Statue Mihály Károlyi's at the Kossuth Square in
  Budapest, was removed in 2009 and-re-erected 2012 in
  Siofok
  Yoav Dothan / Wikimedia Commons / Public Domain

- Mihály Károlyit was elected first President of the
  Republic of Hungary
  Agence de presse Mondial Photo-Presse / Wikimedia
  Commons / Public Domain

Anna Kéthly, A Friend of Social Justice, a Thorn in the Side of Politicians

- Bronze statue on marble base by Benedek Nagy (2015)
  - Széchenyi rakpart, Budapest.
  © user:Globetrotter19 / Wikimedia Commons / CC
  BY-SA 3.0

- The statue of Anna Kéthly in Budapest, Kéthly Anna
  Square
  © Attila Terbócs/ Wikimedia Commons / CC BY-SA
  3.0 / GFDL

- Commemorative plaque of Anna Kéthly in District XIII,
  Pozsonyi Street No 40, Budapest
  © user:Csurla / Wikimedia Commons / CC BY-SA 2.5 /
  GFDL

László Rajk, The Man who was Buried Three Times

- László Rajk during International Workers' Day in 1947
  © Pál Berkó / Wikimedia Commons / CC BY-SA 3.0

- László Rajk's tomb at Kerepesi cementery
  © user: Thaler/ Wikimedia Commons / CC BY-SA 3.0
- Speech at the ceremony of March 15th 1947 at Kossuth Lajos square, Budapest
  © PHOTO:FORTEPAN / Berkó Pál / Wikimedia Commons / CC BY-SA 3.0

Mihály Vörösmarty, The Voice of Despair and Hope

- Portrait of Mihály Vörösmarty (1857)
  Barabás Miklós; Axmann, Josef / Wikimedia Commons / Public Domain
- Bust of Mihály Vörösmarty in Bonyhád (by Szabó György, 1990)
  user: Csanády / Wikimedia Commons / Public Domain
- Statue of Vörösmarty on Vörösmarty tér in Budapest. Sculptors: Ede Kallós and Ede Telcs (1908)
  © Andreas.poeschek / Wikimedia Commons / CC BY-SA 2.0 DE

Franz Liszt, A Lover of Music and Women

- Earliest known photograph of Liszt (1843)
  Herman Biow / Wikimedia Commons / Public Domain
- Liszt in March 1886, four months before his death, photographed by Nadar
  Nadar/ Wikimedia Commons / Public Domain
- Liszt giving a concert for Emperor Franz Joseph I (before 1890)
  / Wikimedia Commons / Public Domain

Tivadar Csontváry, The Painter of Loneliness

- Self-portrait, circa 1896
  Tivadar Csontváry / Wikimedia Commons / Public Domain

- Tomb of Tivadar Csontváry in Budapest, Kerepesi Cemetery: 34/2-1-14
  © Dr Varga József / Wikimedia Commons / CC BY-SA 3.0

- The Lonely Cedar, 1907, Csontváry Museum, Pécs
  Tivadar Csontváry / Wikimedia Commons / Public Domain

Molnár Ferenc, The Bohemian Hungarian Who Conquered Broadway

- Portrait of Ferenc Molnár (1918)
  Ödön Uher/ Wikimedia Commons / Public Domain

- Commemorative plaque on the wall his primary by the artist Johanna Götz
  © Artist: Johanna Götz, Photo: user: Fekist / Wikimedia Commons / CC BY-SA 4.0

- Paul street boys sculpture, Budapest, 8. district, inspired by Molnar's novel: "Paul street boys"
  © Sculptor: Péter Szanyi; Photo: user:misibacsi / Wikimedia Commons / CC BY 3.0 / GFDL

Robert Capa, A Pacifist and Eye-witness to Five Wars

- Gerda Taro (Capa's partner and love) in 1937
  Wikimedia Commons / Public Domain

- Artwork at the birth house of Federico Borrell García; based on Capa's world famous photograph "The Falling Soldier" (the original photograph still under copyright protection in some countries)
  © user:Joanbanjo / Wikimedia Commons / CC BY-SA 4.0

István Örkény, Chronicler of Absurdity

- István Örkény in 1974
  © Ottó Vahl / Wikimedia Commons / CC BY-SA 3.0

- Örkény István's One Minute Stories, depicted by guerilla knitters at Örkény István Theater (Budapest)
  © Elekes Andor / Wikimedia Commons / CC BY-SA 4.0

- Örkény István Theater in Budapest (2016)
  © Elekes Andor / Wikimedia Commons / CC BY-SA 4.0

Zoltán Kodály, The Music Educator of a Nation

- Zoltán Kodály in the 1930s
  Wikimedia Commons / Public Domain

- Zeneakademia (Liszt Academy) Grand Hall, 1942, Zoltán Kodály in the middle
  © PHOTO:FORTEPAN / Lissák Tivadar / Wikimedia Commons / CC BY-SA 3.0

- Budapest Metro (Line 4), Kálvin tér station, the decoration on the wall is a score of Kodály
  © Varius / Wikimedia Commons / CC BY-SA 3.0

Sisi, Queen of the Hungarians

- Elisabeth, Queen of Hungary, Coronation photograph (1867)
  Emil Rabending / Wikimedia Commons / Public Domain

- Sculpture located in St Matthias Church in Budapest, Hungary
  © user: Gebo541 / Wikimedia Commons / CC BY-SA 4.0

- Coronation of Franz Joseph and Elisabeth as Apostolic King and Queen of Hungary in Buda (1867)
  Edmund Tull after Eduard von Engerth/ Wikimedia Commons / Public Domain

Tivadar Herzl, Architect of the Jewish Nation

- Photograph of Tivadar Herzl (circa 1900)
  Carl Pietzner / Wikimedia Commons / Public Domain

- A sketch in Herzl's Diary of a proposed flag for the Zionist movement (1890s)
  Tivadar Herzl / Wikimedia Commons / Public Domain

- Honor guard standing next to Herzel's coffin in Israel
  David Eldan / Wikimedia Commons / Public Domain

Blaha Lujza, The Nation's Nightingale

- Portrait of Blaha Lujza (1866)
  Gondy és Egey / Wikimedia Commons / Public Domain

- Photograph of Blaha Lujza (circa 1902)
  Sándor Strelisky / Wikimedia Commons / Public Domain

- Photograph from the 25th theater performance of the Grandmother (A Nagymama) on the 10th of March, 1908 (Blaha Lujza in the middle)
Strelisky Sándor scanned by an courtesy of Elekes Andor / Wikimedia Commons / Public Domain

Béla Lugosi, The Resurrection of Count Dracula

- Photograph with signature (1912)
© PHOTO:Fortepan / SALY NOÉMI / Wikimedia Commons / CC BY-SA 3.0

- Lugosi's star on Hollywood Walk of Fame
JGKlein / Wikimedia Commons / Public Domain

- A screenshot from Dracula
Wikimedia Commons / Public Domain

Karádi Katalin, Legendary Sex Symbol

- Katalin Karády in 1940
ROZGONYI / Wikimedia Commons / Public Domain

- Another photograph of Karádi Katalin in 1940
Wikimedia Commons / Public Domain

- Commemorative plaque of Katalin Karády in Budapest District V, Nyáry Pál Street No 9
© User:Csurla / Wikimedia Commons / CC BY-SA 2.5

Ferenc Puskás, Everybody's Little Brother

- Puskás at Real Madrid (1960s)
Wikimedia Commons / Public Domain

- Puskás during a football match between Amsterdam and Budapest in 1954

**Móric Benyovszky, The Hungarian Made King of
Madagascar**

Rózsa Sándor, The King of the Betyárs

Ágoston Haraszty,The Father of California Wine

- Portrait of the Hungarian Count Ágoston Haraszthy
  Wikimedia Commons / Public Domain

- Wooden carving from 1889 on the front part of a barrel
  at Buena Vista Winery (still used as the winery's logo)
  Cristalen / Wikimedia Commons / Public Domain

- From Haraszty's book: "Grape culture, wines, and
  wine-making" (1862)
  Ágoston Haraszty / Wikimedia Commons / Public
  Domain

Ignaz Trebitsch, The Talented Mr. Trebitsch

- Portrait from circa 1910-1915
  Wikimedia Commons / Public Domain

- Trebitsch-Lincoln as Chao Kung (1943)
  Wikimedia Commons / Public Domain

László Almássy, The Hungarian Patient

- Portrait of young László Almássy (1915)
  Wikimedia Commons / Public Domain

- Bust of László Almásy in Hungarian Geographical
  Museum, Érd, Hungary
  © Léphaft Áron / Wikimedia Commons / CC BY-SA
  2.5

- "Operation Salaam" at Wadi Sura
  Wikimedia Commons / Public Domain

Arthur Koestler, A Man of Causes

- <u>Photograph of Arthur Koestler in 1969</u>
  © Eric Koch / Anefo / Wikimedia Commons / CC BY-SA 3.0

- <u>1st US edition of Darkness at Noon (Cover)</u>
  Wikimedia Commons / Public Domain

- <u>Arthur Koestler life-size bronze statue sculpted by Imre Varga in Budapest (Városligeti fasor 2)</u>
  © Sculptor: Imre Varga, photo: Derzsi Elekes Andor / Wikimedia Commons / CC BY-SA 3.0

László Bíró, The Man Who Gave His Name to a Pen

- <u>László Bíró on the wall of U4 building in the Graphisoft Park, Budapest (Gázgyár Street)</u>
  © user:Globetrotter19/ Wikimedia Commons / CC BY-SA 3.0

- <u>Advertising in Argentine magazine Leoplán promoting the first commercial ballpoint pen, brand "birome" (1945)</u>
  © user:Roberto Fiadone / Wikimedia Commons / CC BY-SA 2.5

- <u>Commemorative plaque of László Bíró (Budapest District II, Cimbalom utca 12)</u>
  © Csurla / Wikimedia Commons / CC BY-SA 3.0

Albert Szent-györgyi, The Man Behind Vitamin C

- <u>Photograph of Albert Szent-györgyi (1950)</u>
  © PHOTO:FORTEPAN / Semmelweis Egyetem Levéltára / Wikimedia Commons / CC BY-SA 3.0

- Albert Szent-györgyi receives the Nobel Prize (Stockholm 1937)
  Wikimedia Commons / Public Domain

- Szent-györgyi with the formula of Vitamin C in the background (1937)
  Wikimedia Commons / Public Domain

Leo Szilárd, Doctor A-bomb

- Photograph of Leó Szilárd (circa 1960)
  U.S. Department of Energy / Wikimedia Commons / Public Domain

- Atomic Cloud Rises Over Nagasaki (1945)
  Charles Levy / Wikimedia Commons / Public Domain

- The Metallurgical Laboratory scientists, with Szilard third from right, in the lab coat (1946)
  Wikimedia Commons / Public Domain

Pál Erdős, The Vagabond of Mathematics

- Portrait of Pál Erdős in 1992
  © Topsy Kretts / Wikimedia Commons / CC BY-SA 3.0 / GFDL

- Pál Erdős's tomb at the Jewish Cemetery in Budapest, Kozma Street
  © Dr Varga József / Wikimedia Commons / CC BY-SA 3.0

- Paul Erdős teaching 10 year old mathematical child prodigy Terence Tao in 1985, at the University of Adelaide
  © Billy or Grace Tao / Wikimedia Commons / CC BY-SA 2.0

About the Author
Miklós M. Molnár

Linguist, cultural historian and tour guide Miklós M. Molnár spent his first thirty years teaching in higher education, including Budapest's ELTE University and as a Fulbrighter at Rutgers State University, N.J. Later, combining his interests in education and cultural tourism, Miklós went on to found *Fungarian*.

As both an ambassador of the Hungarian language and its culture, keen to disseminate his knowledge and enthusiasm among locals and foreign guests, he was invited to contribute to Time Out Budapest with his popular and successful column 'Magyar of the Month'.

Miklós lives in Budapest, conducting specialised tours of his beloved city – most especially off-the-beaten-track locations, complemented by unique, personal and unforgettable anecdotes.

More about him and Fungarian:

- Video portrait about Miklós M. Molnár on YouTube: www.bit.ly/MiklosMolnar
- www.fungarian.com
- www.edtourshungary.com
- www.facebook.com/fungarian

About the Publisher
Catch Budapest

Juli and Flo are a Hungarian-Austrian couple living in Budapest. After traveling the world together for several months they both decided to devote their time to what they love most: Exploring and getting under the surface of their surroundings and living their city to the fullest. On Catch Budapest they write about all their discoveries and explorations in the Hungarian capital and encourage their readers to make the most of their time in Budapest.

Visit their site www.CatchBudapest.com to read more about their books and publishing. You will also find plenty of awesome information and articles about life and language in Budapest and you can even sign up for their newsletter so that you're always first to hear about new blog articles and releases.

You can also find them on facebook and Instagram.

Plus they are always happy if you say hello at hello@catchbudapest.com.

Printed in Poland
by Amazon Fulfillment
Poland Sp. z o.o., Wrocław